PLANTING WITH PURPOSE

Planting With Purpose

How Farmers Create a Resilient Food Landscape

Stephen Ellingson

NEW YORK UNIVERSITY PRESS
New York

NEW YORK UNIVERSITY PRESS
New York
www.nyupress.org

© 2024 by New York University
All rights reserved

Library of Congress Cataloging-in-Publication Data
Names: Ellingson, Stephen, 1962– author.
Title: Planting with purpose : how farmers create a resilient food landscape / Stephen Ellingson.
Description: New York : New York University Press, [2024] | Includes bibliographical references and index.
Identifiers: LCCN 2023019347 | ISBN 9781479820641 (hardback) | ISBN 9781479820665 (paperback) | ISBN 9781479820672 (ebook) | ISBN 9781479820719 (ebook other)
Subjects: LCSH: Local foods—United States. | Farms, Small—United States. | Sustainable agriculture—United States. | Food supply—United States—Moral and ethical aspects.
Classification: LCC HD9005 .E45 2024 | DDC 338.1/973—dc23/eng/20230421
LC record available at https://lccn.loc.gov/2023019347

This book is printed on acid-free paper, and its binding materials are chosen for strength and durability. We strive to use environmentally responsible suppliers and materials to the greatest extent possible in publishing our books.

Manufactured in the United States of America

10 9 8 7 6 5 4 3 2 1

Also available as an ebook

For Mesafint

CONTENTS

1. What Is Local Food and Why Is It Important?	1
2. The Moral Foundations of Local Food Production	41
3. Building the Local Foodshed	87
4. Morality, Emotions, and the Future of Local Food	125
Acknowledgments	161
Appendix: Study Participants	163
Notes	165
References	177
Index	189
About the Author	197

1

What Is Local Food and Why Is It Important?

It was a typical midwinter day in central New York—well below freezing, snow swirling, gray clouds hanging low in the sky. The weather was bleak, and my conversation with Laura Donovan, co-owner of Quiet Springs Farm, had just turned bleak as well. I had asked her about the challenges she faced getting her small organic beef and lamb farm established, and she poured out a tale of hardships and frustrations. High costs, no economies of scale, limited infrastructure to support small farmers, and a consumer base accustomed to the low meat prices found in conventional grocery stores. All of this suggested that small-scale local farming was not easy or very sustainable:

> I think scale is the biggest problem. You know, we're not big enough to sell at wholesale. . . . So then you can produce it, you can keep track of your costs and you can sell to cover them, but are you pricing yourself out of your market? You can't let the local market drive your price because then you just race to the bottom. . . . We usually charge more than anybody else because that's what it costs me. So we still qualify for food stamps; we don't use them but we qualify.

Laura's comments about high costs, low profitability, and the unfairness built into American agriculture mirrored those of other farmers I interviewed. Fundamentally, her lament gets at the endemic uncertainty under which farmers labor. Weather, rising costs for seed, equipment, and labor, and the fickleness of the market create an uncertain environment for farmers.[1] For example, Scott Wilson farms 106 acres (mostly leased), down from 170 acres originally, on which he grows a wide variety of grains and produce. He hoped to capitalize on the booming commodity market for corn and soybeans, but events out of his control crushed that hope. He could not anticipate the policy moves in Washington nor the back-to-back hundred-year floods that would drive him to the edge of bankruptcy:

> I didn't figure it was going to drop to an all-time forty-year low because of some policy decisions make in DC. I'll just put it this way: sanctions that they say are to harm another country usually harm the country who imposes the sanctions.... And unfortunately, the sanction item was grain. When you take out 50 percent of your trading ability, your price is going to drop more than 50 percent. And it hasn't come back.... Then in 2013 we had the flood. We planted our grain crop three times. I lost almost $450,000 that year, which is three times my yearly income.... In '14 I got nailed again with a flood. Two years in a row, we got hit.... It took its toll. And as part of the toll you downsize, you get rid of land, you get rid of crops that are not making money, and you adjust down to the point where you either can't afford to do it or you barely get by. I'm barely getting by. I lose money on most every crop we grow today.

The accounts of both of these central New York farmers raise the questions, Why does someone enter the local food market? And what sustains them through the difficult challenges of making a farm viable? Becoming a small-scale, local farmer does not appear to be a decision based on a rational calculation of costs and benefits, nor is there a magic bullet for the business model that will make it all work. Simply discovering the right seeds, cultivating fertile soil, and developing a loyal set of buyers are no guarantees of market success. While business models and good seed certainly help, I found that participants in central New York's local food market enter and remain involved in spite of risk, loss, and low earnings because they are committed to a set of values and practices that define a good life. In this book, I show how farmers, chefs, and artisanal food producers create a moral order that guides their work. This moral order is based on a shared set of beliefs about sustainability and stewardship, health and risk, cooperation and competition, relationships and family. These beliefs and values engender emotions and assessments of the self that together motivate a commitment to local foods and help them weather the uncertainties of farming.

This focus on morality emerged as I read some of the initial interview transcripts with farmers and chefs. I began the study hoping to learn how individuals got involved working in the local food system. I wanted to learn about their jobs and how they met the challenges of producing food in a small and emerging market. Surprisingly, almost every one of my fifty-one interviewees talked about the deep values that gave their work meaning. Their answers to my questions about how they got involved in local food or what they found challenging and rewarding were peppered with terms such as "stewardship," "care for the earth," or "building community." They spoke passionately about the relationships they had forged with customers and one another, about their drive to alleviate climate change, and about how values such as honesty, transparency, and cooperation influenced their work. The language my interviewees used suggested that they thought about the local food market in more than economic or instrumental terms, and that I should attend to the moral dimensions of local food production.

In addition, decisions about the production, distribution, and consumption of food are at root moral ones. Fundamentally the production, distribution, and consumption of food pose critical questions about risk and harm and the meaning of the good person, the good community, or the good life. The claims we make about food regarding health, risk, price, sustainability, and taste are, at root, moral because they key into values that govern human relationships such as mutuality, transparency, trust, and respect. They also articulate, even if inchoately, "what people care about in the first place" and thus reflect "an orientation towards what is right and wrong, good and bad, worthy and unworthy."[2] Moreover, by treating food as a commodity, we create moral dilemmas about access, security, fairness, and inequality. The scholarly literature about food often discusses the moral issues connected to it, but at times does so obliquely or focuses on the ethics of consumption. Some researchers identify the connection between food and the care we provide for families and friends, and they suggest that food is tied up in the prosaic morality of parenting and care work.[3] Much of the literature about community-supported agriculture (CSA) and farmers' markets emphasizes how alternative food markets are places to rebuild community and build relationships of transparency and trust, and thus pushes us to think about how food and civic norms are interrelated.[4] Some agrifood scholars argue that farming itself is a form of care work insofar as it is focused on one or more of three sets of ethical practices: "*first*, care for local economies, environments and future generations; *second*, care for health and wholeness; and *finally*, care about transparency and integrity in food systems."[5]

The literature on "ethical consumption" highlights how shoppers' moral commitments to justice, health, biodiversity, and ecological sustainability motivate decisions to purchase local and/or organic food.[6] Sage contrasts "bad" and "good" in their study of alterative food networks in Ireland. They note that bad food

> encompasses homogenized food produced without due consideration of the naturalness, provenance, and quality of its ingredients, food which has not been produced with the high regard for animal welfare, the environment and the nutritional well-being of its consumers. . . . Good food, then, constitutes a dialectical alternative: food which is authentic, derivative of a place or person(s), produced with regard to principles of sustainability, naturalness and animal welfare; food which is not only nutritionally sound, which is good to eat, but also, following Levi-Strauss's famous dictum, food that is "good to think."[7]

One goal of this book is to move the focus of the analysis away from the well-studied phenomenon of ethical consumption and place it on the moral grounding of production. In particular, I aim to show how those who grow or produce food construct a moral order to guide their participation in local markets. Much of the scholarship about local food focuses on specific types of producers (e.g., community-supported agriculture farms), but rarely on how the various actors collectively organize the local food system around a shared moral vision. A second goal of the book is to contribute to the growing literature about the sociology of morality, and, more specifically, to rehabilitate a theory of action that takes morality as a critical factor that motivates, sustains, and alters how people enter and engage in local food production.

The Emergence and Growth of Local Food Systems

"The term [local food] generally refers to agricultural products, such as fruit, vegetables, meat, and cheese, that are minimally processed and grown near the final point of sale."[8] Local food has become an increasingly popular and financially important part of American agriculture. According to a 2015 USDA report about local foods,

> Consumer, producer, and policymaker interest in local foods appears to be growing. Farm operations with direct-to-consumer (DTC) sales of food for human consumption increased from 116,733 to 144,530 between 2002 and 2012. Consumers have more opportunities to purchase food directly from producers, with 8,268 farmers' markets operating in 2014, up 180 percent since 2006. . . . The growing interest in local foods in the United States is the result of consumer interest in environmental and community concerns (where community concerns include supporting local farmers and the local economy but also increasing access to healthful foods).

The number of farmers' markets, a critical site for the sale of local foods in the United States, has increased fivefold, from 1,755 in 1994 to 8,771 in 2019. The same 2015 report also identifies significant increases in the number of farm-to-school programs, food hubs (cooperative enterprises to distribute local foods to larger markets), and sales to restaurants, as well as growing state-level policy and legislative support for community gardens, urban agriculture, and the expansion of farmers' markets.[9] According to the USDA, there are more than 4,500 CSAs, another primary avenue for the sale of local produce and meat (Local Harvest reported over 5,600 CSAs in 2015). The National Restaurant Association's Hot Chef Survey from 2014 indicates that "locally sourced meats and seafood" and "locally grown produce" are ranked numbers one and two respectively on the top ten list of menu trends.[10]

Over the past ten to fifteen years there has been a shift in production toward small local farms and CSAs, with a growing set of new young farmers and artisanal producers across the eight counties that comprise the study region of central New York. According to the Local Harvest web page, there are 124 CSAs or other small local food producers in these counties, along with 17 farmers markets.[11] This is a surprising development insofar as many of these counties are made up of agriculturally dense areas (with few large metropolitan centers) that have historically been tied to conventional agriculture, especially dairy. According to the 2017 USDA Agricultural Census, dairy remains the dominant form of agriculture in central New York: milk sales accounts for 76–88 percent of all agricultural sales in the region, and the vast majority of acres (70–90 percent) in each of the eight counties is dedicated to growing hay or corn for animal feed.[12] It is also a region that has a small upper-middle-class population, typically identified as the most likely set of consumers who participate in local food markets (the median income ranges between $47,000 and $54,000; on average 21 percent of the population has a college education, 15.7 percent of the population falls below the poverty line, and unemployment since 2000 has ranged between 4 and 12 percent).[13] The infrastructure for local foods is underdeveloped and in some cases absent altogether. There are no food hubs or distributors in the counties of the study; three food stores that specialized in local food closed; and another never advanced beyond the planning stage during the study period. Small-scale local food producers face greater risk, higher costs, and narrower profit margins than conventional producers, and they must help create their own market.

In addition to a rapidly growing set of new farmers, there is an emerging array of artisanal products crafted and available in the area—cheesemakers, craft breweries and distilleries, bakeries. Their products are no doubt part of what some are calling an "artisanal renaissance" in the United States, in which entrepreneurs are establishing craft breweries, distilleries, and creameries at a record pace. Recent work has linked the emergence of artisanal food in large cities to the rediscovery of lost craft production and the histories of specific places, and to intentional efforts to challenge the hegemony of corporate commodity food production.[14] Again, central New York does not have a particularly large or vibrant foodie subculture, and yet local foods seem to be thriving.

Central New York is a latecomer to the local food movement. The roots can be traced back to the counterculture's "back to the land" movement of the late 1960s and 1970s, when Americans became more aware and concerned about the safety of their food supply due to the application of chemical pesticides, herbicides, and fertilizers, along with a growing ecological consciousness cultivated by the emergent environmental movement. Activists criticized industrial and corporate agriculture for prioritizing profits over safety, convenience over taste, artificial over natural products.[15] Although the counterculture waned, the impetus to challenge the industrial food system, along with a more general mistrust of faceless bureaucracies, government, and institutions, did not. During the 1980s and 1990s the concerns of a variety of groups (activists, consumers, scholars) and the expanding globalization of food production and distribution converged to catalyze a widespread move to embrace local food. Lapping argues that the three pillars of the contemporary American food system—globalization, corporate consolidation, and industrialization—pushed many small farmers off their land, created tasteless produce and a massive market for processed foods whose quality and health benefits were questionable, and threatened to undermine the safety of food. He writes, "Fears about the introduction of artificial hormones into dairy products, outbreaks of salmonella in fast and other processed foods, incidents of mad-cow disease in beef cattle herds, and other health-related problems have led many to question both the current direction of American food policy and the food system itself."[16]

The problems associated with industrial and global agriculture also created widespread distrust of the food system. One response was the development of the organic market, but its co-optation by corporate food giants and the challenges associated with certification for farmers discredited organics for some and deepened the push for a more transparent locally based agricultural system. Food scholar and activist Michael Mikulak speaks to the growing mistrust of corporate organics and green labeling of food:

> Today's organic food is a response to a consumer- and producer-driven moment that has emerged as part of a broader environmental consciousness and anxiety about toxicity, health, and the deleterious effects of industrial agriculture. Advertisers have cleverly tapped into this anxiety with green marketing. . . . Despite consumer willingness to pay premiums for green products, the lack of transparency can easily lead to cynicism, as the words "natural," "green," and "eco-" appear on products that clearly do not embrace the ideals they conjure up.[17]

Mikulak also identifies a second force pushing for local food production, namely, environmental consciousness. Concerns about the polluting effects of the chemicals used in agriculture, the deleterious effects on soil and plant health from giant monocrop farms, and the role the global transportation of food plays in climate change have fueled a desire for more local foods. This is most commonly seen in the scholarly and popular writings about "food miles" (how far food must travel from producer to consumer). The assumption is that the shorter the distance the food must travel, the lower the impact of greenhouse gas emissions.[18] In one study of "buy local" initiatives in the United States, one-third of the claims made to justify these initiatives focused on the environmental benefits of consuming local food: reduced energy use and lowered pollution levels from shorter travel of food to markets, reduced packaging, and preservation of farmland.[19]

Finally, local food became tied to taste and quality. In California a new wave of chefs and restauranteurs emerged during the 1970s and 1980s, best known by Alice Waters's restaurant, Chez Panisse. They were creating a new American cuisine based on locally sourced and seasonal ingredients. Chefs looking to promote fresh ingredients, healthy food, and conviviality around the table sought out nearby farmers and foragers, cheesemakers, and butchers who could provision their restaurants with superior ingredients.[20] DeLind claims that for health-conscious consumers, local food has become integrated into self-improvement projects because local is "understood to be fresher, riper, more nutritious, and thus a healthier product than its long-distance counterpart. The relative absence of food miles, likewise, makes it possible to avoid the compromising demands of extended shelf life, transport, packaging, and/or synthetic re-fortification."[21] In many ways, the benefits offered by local food promised to meet the interests and needs of a variety of stakeholders, from environmentalists to ethical consumers, from the health-conscious to upscale foodies, from defenders of local economies to critics of big business. Writing about community-supported agriculture, Thompson and Press note that the appeal of local food is grounded in its promise of "enhancing biodiversity, revitalizing local economies and the economic viability of small farms, reclaiming food production from corporate-dominated agribusiness interests, and rekindling communal connections that have been weakened by forces of suburbanization, increased geographic mobility and the privatizing influences of consumer culture."[22]

Despite a great deal of scholarly and journalistic writing about local food, there is no single shared definition of what the phenomenon means. For example, one 2006 study of Washington State consumers and farmers found that the meanings of "local" were too varied to draw any conclusions about what local food means in terms of its practices, scale, or scope.[23] Proximity and space are central criteria for how consumers and farmers determine what counts as local, but there is little consensus. Some consider food local if it meets a relatively small geographic range (such as a 25–100-mile radius), while others operate with more expansive understandings that may include a county, state, or multi-state watershed. The ambiguity about the meaning of local food stems from the needs and interests of actors in different roles (e.g., chef versus home shopper) and the environment regarding the availability of foods based on growing region or agricultural infrastructure (e.g., there are few wines made from locally grown grapes east of Syracuse, due to the climate, nor are there many food hubs that serve as central marketplaces for local foods in central New York).

However, there are a core set of production and distribution institutions and a shared set of values or ideals held by many participants that set local food apart from conventional or industrial agriculture. The former includes farmers' markets and farm stands, food hubs, CSAs, community and rooftop gardens, food co-ops and organic grocery stores, farm-to-table restaurants, small-scale artisanal food producers (cheesemakers, meat producers, bakers, "farm" breweries and distilleries), "niche" farms (e.g., farms that produce only grass-fed beef or microgreens for salads), and "micro" farms (farms under five acres that grow a diverse set of crops).

These diverse actors share a number of values, ideals, or assumptions about local food. First, small-scale is superior because it can promote the formation of community as it facilitates direct contact between farmers and consumers. The heightened degree of direct contact pushes farmers to be more transparent about how they produce crops, tend their animals, and more generally guarantee the safety of their products. Thus, consumers may hold farmers accountable to follow such moral imperatives. Second, producers believe that if local food is grown in a more ecologically sustainable manner, then it will be fresher, more nutritious, and tastier. In addition, producers may share a set of attributes that run counter to those who work in industrial agriculture and that are prized by local food consumers: autonomy, lower reliance on chemicals; higher degree of inter-farmer cooperation; a desire to preserve historic farmlands and farm traditions; a commitment to promote biodiversity; and a willingness to prioritize social and ecological values over profit.[24] These ideas and beliefs about local food arise, in part, from the national discourse about local foods.

The Stories behind the Local Food Movement

The emergence and growth of local food would not have been possible without the efforts of journalists, activists, and others to create a set of narratives that promoted its culinary, health, environmental, and moral virtues. Numerous scholars have identified the central role food writing plays in the development of new foodways and the justification for the production and consumption of different types of foods or cuisines. In her study of how French cuisine developed during the nineteenth century, Ferguson notes that "gastronomic texts were the key agents in the socialization of individual desire and the redefinition of appetite in collective terms. The 'second-order' culinary consumption of textual appreciation was as crucial for the construction of the gastronomic field as it was (and is) for its operation."[25] Similarly, in their work about contemporary foodie discourse, Johnston and Baumann show how food writing (from cooking magazines to blogs to books) creates the boundaries that define good and bad food, legitimates agricultural and culinary practices, and offers the public ways to understand the aesthetic, political, and moral nature of food. They note that "gastronomy, and indeed all cultural fields, is textually constructed. Gastronomy must be understood not simply as a fixed set of culinary practices, but as a fluid discursive field where the legitimacy of food production and consumption methods are negotiated."[26] The stories we tell about food are important because they help members of the public see which foods they should eat, what the appropriate methods for producing food are, and which types of producers they should support.

But what makes stories about local food compelling, and compelling enough to shift the production and consumption practices that have fueled the emergence of an alternative food system? To answer this, we must understand how stories work in general and consider the accounts writers offer to persuade eaters to adopt a diet full of locally sourced food.

Stories work at the cognitive and emotional levels by providing humans with the means to make sense of the world and their experiences and by signaling how we should feel. Scholars who study stories have identified how they work as sense-making devices. First, stories present us with the world as it is and/or as it ought to be and thus help us explain both the familiar and the unfamiliar. Mayer argues that "by putting our experience into stories, inevitably we are explaining why things happen," and that we use narratives to make a disorderly world understandable by pegging it to plots, characters, relationships, and outcomes that we already know.[27] Smith suggests that stories explain the world, events, or human motivations by answering questions of who, what, when, how, and why. In doing this, "narratives allocate causal responsibility for action, define actors and give them motivation, indicate the trajectory of past episodes, predict consequences of future choices, suggest course of action, confer and withdraw legitimacy, and provide social approval by aligning events with normative cultural codes."[28] Narratives operate most powerfully when they condense or elide information because they encourage the listener or reader to draw on their own knowledge of narrative conventions, experiences of social institutions, relationships, and taken-for-granted information about society. The use of the term "pasture-raised" (left undefined) in a story about a local farmer is meaningful for some because it relies on a set of knowledge about alternative and conventional agriculture, assumptions about healthy and unhealthy food, and images of an idyllic farm where cattle chew contentedly knee-deep in lush green grass. Thus, stories encourage audiences to become active meaning makers by leaving gaps that we can fill, as well as by providing us with new and not-so-new ways of understanding and explaining reality.

Second, stories are intended to make a point or provide a lesson, to legitimate some identities and delegitimate others, and more broadly to affirm particular worldviews. This is how they create, sustain, and challenge the normative or moral order of a community. Polletta remarks that

> when you tell a story about your firm, or a particular repair job, or your recently married friends, your audience hears the story as having larger implications—about the culture of this firm, or what it is to be a copier repairperson, or the trials facing the newly married. The story of how a particular marriage went wrong *is implicitly a story of how a marriage should work.*[29]

In other words, stories offer models of how to behave in particular situations and relationships. They also tell us who are worthy and unworthy types of actors (note how stories are filled with "types" of characters—heroes, victims, villains, fools, and wise souls), and they often tell us what goes wrong when characters fail to meet social expectations or follow the rules.[30] Ultimately, stories "tell us who we are, where we are, what we are, why we are here, what we should do, and why it all matters."[31]

Third, stories evoke emotions or even provide us with an education in emotions, and the triggering of emotions may compel us to act. By explaining troubling events, by prefiguring ways to resolve social conflict, and by affirming collectively held values, stories' sense-making and didactic functions can both cause us to experience specific emotions and tell us what we ought to feel. For example, "stories of exodus, revolution, foes vanquished, and threats averted strengthen national identities by stimulating emotions of fear, pride, longing replaced by determination, and grief replaced by joy."[32] Stories will be more likely to trigger emotions when we are able to see ourselves in the characters or identity with them, when the plot affirms deeply held values, or when the story shows us a way to resolve persistent social dilemmas we face. More pointedly, to the degree that stories about food align with our values about health or taste, or saving the planet or our local economy, they will be more likely to trigger strong emotions such as anger and outrage over the toxic effects of pesticides or pride in knowing that one has helped lessen greenhouse emissions by supporting local agriculture.

Narratives about local food are grounded in the decades-old discourse about alternative foods that includes several common themes: critiques of the industrial food system that raise alarms about food safety and health along with its attending environmental costs; invocations of American pastoralism that call for a return to an idyllic rural foodscape in which farmer and consumer build small communities based on honesty, trust, and a shared commitment to changing the food system through market decisions; and accounts of the superior quality, taste, and freshness of local food often found in the travelogues and restaurant reviews of gourmet food writing. Across a variety of story types, writers couch these themes in the language of morality, in which food choices are how we can produce the good agricultural system, the good diet, and the good life.[33]

Johnston and Baumann note that the broad alternative food discourse often focuses on environmental concerns and community building, while ignoring other issues such as food security or the rights and safety of agricultural workers. Well-known champions of local, organic, and sustainable agriculture such as *New York Times* columnist Mark Bittman, authors Barbara Kingsolver and Michael Pollan, and chef Alice Waters often link local food production and consumption as the means to ameliorate climate change, preserve or conserve farmland, and eliminate endemic health problems such as obesity, diabetes, and heart disease.[34] The earliest and most common justification for local foods emphasized how it can shorten the number of miles food must travel and thus minimize fuel costs and greenhouse gas emissions. A common story type in which solutions are offered to the environmental and health problems caused by the industrial food system is the "commodity biography," which aims "to reveal the ways in which modern food production systematically conceals environmental damage, health effects, and the exploitation of animals, labourers, and farmers."[35]

The writings of Michael Pollan rely on this genre; many of his works highlight how local foods become the way to resolve the myriad problems of industrial agriculture. For example, in a 2006 *New York Times* essay, he claims that local food will improve human health and lessen the effects of climate change: "[local] food is generally fresher, and in produce, fresher means tastier and more nutritious. . . . Local food generally leaves a much lighter environmental footprint. The average fruit or vegetable on the American plate has traveled 1,500 miles from the farm, and a lot of diesel fuel has been burned to get it there. Local food has much lower energy costs."[36] In his best-selling book *The Omnivore's Dilemma*, Pollan devotes a chapter to one of the pioneering local meat producers in the United States, Joel Salatin's Polyface Farm. He follows the short routes the farm's meat takes to reach consumers, assuming that "Joel's motive for keeping his food chain short was strictly environmental," but he learns that the owner also aims to build relationships of trust between farmer and consumers (and thus develop some sense of community) and to turn the act of local farming and eating into "an act of social, environmental, nutritional, and political redemption."[37] Here Pollan frames the benefits of local food in quasi-religious language, thus elevating its production and consumption into acts of moral courage.

A year later Pollan sharpened his defense of local food as he attacked the industrial food system and its partners, nutrition science and processed food companies. In the new book, *In Defense of Food*, he focuses on the post–World War II food system and the "Western Diet," which have led to profound negative health effects on Americans. The kinds of foods we routinely purchase in the supermarket, he contends, only appear to be nutritious and healthy. Instead, he presents a manifesto to eat "real" (i.e., not processed) food, and argues that local food purchased via farmers' markets, CSAs, or even one's own garden would be

> a simple act with a host of profound consequences for your health, as well as for the health of the food chain as a whole. . . . Local produce is typically picked ripe and is fresher than supermarket produce, and for those

reasons it should be tastier and more nutritious. . . . To survive in the farmers' market or CSA economy, a farm will need to be highly diversified, and a diversified farm usually has little need for pesticides.[38]

Pollan's defense of local food combines warnings about the negative environmental and health effects of industrial food with the promise that local food will be healthier and tastier, and that it will restore transparency, trust, and community bonds between farmer and consumer.

In my own analysis of food journalism since the early 2000s, I found two other types of stories that justify and celebrate local foods: the food memoir and the pioneer story.[39] Both types of accounts aim to persuade readers to support local foods by explaining the reasons why local food is a better option than conventionally farmed produce and meat and the prepared foods Michael Pollan rails against in *In Defense of Food*. The memoirs range from coming-of-age tales narrated by small farmers or chefs to writers who report on their year of trying to follow the hundred-mile diet. "Pioneer" stories focus on different kinds of local food protagonists, such as the creative locavore chef who sources nearly all of his food locally, or the forager who introduces chefs and consumers to produce that is hidden but available in their own backyards. They are cast in the role of hero, innovator, or pioneer whose daring actions promise to offer consumers healthy food, revitalize the local economy, or save the family farm.[40] Both types of narrative personalize local food either by showing how it is possible and rewarding to eat locally, and/or by helping readers understand the world of the farmer and decide to support their work. Such narratives offer eaters moral and emotional reasons to adopt a diet rich in locally sourced foods.

The memoirs, especially those about a writer's experience with following a local and/or seasonal diet, read like travelogues, but here the journey is inward rather than to distant lands. These accounts usually point toward or conclude with some personal transformation the author experienced. One of the first local food memoirs is Gary Nabhan's *Coming Home to Eat*, in which he describes the joys and challenges of eating only foods grown within a 250-mile radius of his home in Tucson, Arizona. The book is organized by the four seasons and he takes the reader on a tour of his home garden, on his foraging trips for wild greens and mushrooms, and on visits with local farmers to learn about ancient varieties of corn and chilies. Nabhan's year of eating locally was motivated by both environmental and aesthetic concerns as he hoped to opt out of the "transnational vending machine" (i.e., the industrial global food system and processed food industries) and come to deeply understand who grows his food and how they do so:

> The markets are being flooded with nutraceutical, transgenic foods, irradiated grains and other such marginally edible gobbled-gook. A handful of companies control the bulk of the global food economy. . . . Most of them are unwilling to tell us whether our food crops have been sprayed with toxins in the old-fashioned way, or ingeniously modified genetically to produce the same toxins. . . . As conscientious consumers, we are told that we should be preoccupied with issues regarding the chemical composition, the days since initial packaging, and the densities of insect parts and fecal coliform found in the grains ground down to make our daily bread. Nonetheless we don't much fathom from whom or from whence they came.[41]

Nabhan's memoir articulates the themes that will animate local food writing for the next twenty years as it combines a critique of industrial agriculture with the pleasures of discovering healthy, tasty new foods and building ties to the previously hidden farming community. At the end of the book, as he reflects on his year, the author connects eating locally with religious or spiritual imperatives, thus bolstering the instrumental rationale with a moral one:

> If we no longer believe that the earth is sacred, or that we are blessed by the bounty around us, or that we have a caretaking responsibility given to us by the Creator . . . then it does not really matter to most folks how

much ecological and cultural damage is done by the way we eat. It does not matter whether we ever participate in the butchering of our meat, the harvesting and grinding of our grain, the foraging and drying of our herbs. Until we stop craving to be somewhere else and someone else other than animals whose very cells are constituted from the place on earth we love the most, then there is little reason to care about the fate of native foods, family farms, or health landscapes and communities.[42]

In its early days, then, the literature about American local food was linked to distinctly moral ends—stewardship of the land, conserving indigenous foodways, protecting health, and restoring the natural world. These ideals are repeated by many who followed Nabhan's quest for and commitment to local foods, and, as will be evident in chapter 2, they also are invoked as motivations for some of the farmers I interviewed.

Just a few years later, environmentalist Bill McKibben penned his own local food memoir. In "A Grand Experiment" he charts his seven-month effort to eat locally. He begins the essay by musing about the challenges of eating locally in an international food system in which much of what Americans eat travels 1,500 miles, and wonders whether "local" and "seasonal" are simply buzzwords, or whether it is possible to eat locally in a northern climate such as Vermont. He previews the outcome at the end of the first paragraph: "I'm writing this, so you know I survived. But, in fact, I survived in style—it was the best eating winter of my life." In the rest of the essay, he offers short summaries of how he successfully navigated a local diet each month and writes about specific features of local food. In September, for example, he introduces the important practice of home canning as he stocks up on produce for the winter; while in his entry for October he describes how the local grain milling industry in the state fuels his foray into baking. He provides short vignettes of local farmers, and describes the culinary joys provided by Vermont's apples, cheese, and beer producers. Like Pollan, he also aims to show how industrialized agriculture can damage small rural communities and create significant environmental problems like toxic waste lagoons of large-scale pork producers that threaten the integrity of groundwater. Along the way he makes the argument that eating locally is both good for the environment and tasty, and concludes with the following lesson:

> Look—eating this way has come at a cost. Not in health, or in money (if anything I've spent less than I usually would since I haven't bought a speck of processed foods), but in time. I've had to think about every meal, instead of cruising through the world on autopilot, ingesting random calories. I've had to pay attention. But the payoff for that cost has been immense, a web of connections I'd never have known about otherwise. Sure, I'm looking forward to the occasional banana, the odd pint of Guinness stout. But I think this winter has permanently altered the way I eat.[43]

Thus, McKibben's locavore journey has transformed him in ways he did not expect, which is the surprise at the heart of the story as well as the promise that it could happen for readers. The way in which his experiment altered his sense of time and induced a sort of mindfulness is the unanticipated bonus of the locavore diet. In addition, he identifies the various ways in which a diet based on local foods is a moral and social good: it promotes health; it is better for the environment if for no other reason than promoting biodiversity; it is unexpectedly cheaper than buying non-local foods; and it creates community.

Some writers offer a more critical approach to the hundred-mile diet, in which they document their struggles to figure out what "local" means (can one eat a restaurant meal if the spices are not produced locally?) and how to abide by the lack of variability and culinary restrictions imposed by a local diet. In the essay "Miles to Go before I Eat," Mark Anderson quickly discovers that the downsides of eating locally—from incurring costly purchases (sixty dollars for a bottle of California olive oil), to the socially awkward grilling of vendors at farmers' markets to determine whether their produce conforms to his draconian one-mile limit—are outweighed by the benefits. He notes how good he feels to support farmers who engage in sustainable practices, and how much healthier his diet became. And like McKibben, he finds that the surprises of eating a locavore diet transformed his views about food. Originally, he set out to eat locally for one week, but his experiences inspired him to commit to eating locally. He concludes by explaining his reasons for this decision:

> The inherently intriguing stories behind the milk and honey, the bacon and eggs, the apples and onions allow for another layer of flavor I didn't necessarily anticipate. With food playing such a fundamental role in our day-to-day existence and basic social-cultural experience—in a world where we are increasingly isolated from our food by monsoon-proof packaging and intercontinental processing and shipping—it tastes damn good to step outside the industrial food complex and personally know the nexus of my nourishment.[44]

Memoirs such as these aim to demystify local food by showing how easy and rewarding it is to eat locally. The defense of local foods is made on moral, aesthetic, and ecological grounds. As a result, answering the call to follow in the footsteps of the hundred-mile experimenters places the reader on the moral and culinary high ground. Perhaps more importantly, this type of story also gives readers a promise of the emotional benefits of eating locally—that is, the joy that comes from eating tastier produce and supporting the local economy.

In the pioneer story, farmers, chefs, ranchers, and foragers often are identified as heroes, and placed in a comedic plot in which they struggle to overcome the economic challenges of running a local food business, or, through entrepreneurial genius, develop the infrastructure and market to make local food a success.[45] This mode of emplotment tends to heighten the powers, legitimacy, and moral virtues of the protagonists. The food pioneers are depicted as deeply motivated by moral ideals: saving the land and the environment, rebuilding community, preserving health. Moreover, the aim in many of the pioneer stories is to illustrate how the conventional food system or industrial agriculture can be reformed or overturned. Ultimately, the pioneer story is one that combines elements of the "Horatio Alger" tale (i.e., the self-made person), redemption myths, the underdog or comeback story of sports, and the narrative of the hero who restores community and order.

For example, John Kessler's essay "The Upstart Cattleman" tells the story of how a Georgia rancher who inherited the family ranch turned his back on conventional ranching. The article begins by describing the set of old and new ranching practices that carry the weight of the kind of moral critique of industrial agriculture made in Rachel Carson's *Silent Spring* and more recently in the works of Michael Pollan:[46]

> One day, without consulting anyone he just stopped. He stopped feeding his cattle a mixed ration of grain and powdered dietary supplements they digested poorly, and he stopped implanting estrogen pellets behind their ears. He stopped buying bull semen and instead bought bulls. He stopped loading weaned 7-month-old calves into 53-foot-long double-decker hauling trucks to travel 1,400 miles in their own filth to a feedlot. Soon, he stopped spraying his pasture with pesticides and fertilizing them with ammonium nitrate, and as they turned brown and died, he knew he was risking everything. But he kept going.[47]

The rest of the story chronicles how he came to this decision and then how he transformed his farm into a key beef supplier to restaurants and Whole Foods Market in the Atlanta metro region. The transformation began with a reading of Wendell Berry's *The Unsettling of America*, which caused him to think deeply about the kind of agriculture he and his family had been practicing, what kind of legacy he wanted to pass along to his daughters, and just how wrong it was to "send 80 calves off in a double-decker hauling truck with urine and excrement raining down" on those on the bottom. A dinner with a Slow Food group in Atlanta shaped his thinking about both a new market for his beef and how to raise cattle in a more humane and sustainable manner. After a multimillion-dollar loan and a few lean years while his pastures recovered from the years of chemicals, he began to turn a profit. By 2013, the rancher was selling $20 million annually in naturally raised meat, and pumped $2.3 million into the local economy.[48] Here is a powerful lesson of how growing food for the local market in a sustainable manner saved the farm and the animals, and kept a small-town economy afloat.

While some pioneer stories focus on a hero who overcomes the economic and logistical problems of operating a local food business, others highlight ordinary people who hope to produce healthier, tastier food, foster community, or build the local economy. These "less-than-heroic" articles take the reader into a restaurant kitchen as chefs describe the relationships they have forged with area farmers and artisanal producers to create locavore menus, on walking tours of the bucolic pastures of CSAs, or behind the tables at busy farmers' markets. In such accounts we read about the Bay Area forager who starts up the first "community-supported forage" business; the home cook who decides to follow the hundred-mile diet and finds their cooking and life transformed; or the second-career family who start up a local berry patch and can't keep up with demand.

A good example of this variation of the pioneer story is from a recent *Food & Wine* article featuring a James Beard Award-winning chef, Spike Gjerde. The reporter first describes the meal the chef served for the opening of a new restaurant and then details where the ingredients come from. The author describes him as a chef who "has approached local sourcing with religious fervor. He forgoes olive oil and lemons, using locally grown and pressed oils and vinegars in their place. His team dries mint, lavender, peaches, and cherries. . . . He refuses to buy from distributors, even when they buy from local growers, because he wants every penny to go to the farm." He seeks out new producers, teaches them how to work with restaurants and create viable business plans for his partners. The article then ends with short vignettes of eight of his suppliers—from oysterman and cider mill, to organic orchardist and salt maker—who form a community of like-minded foodies committed to making alternative agriculture work so we won't "have corn and soy as far as the eye can see."[49]

The pioneer story grounds its defense of local food on the appealing traits and virtuous motivations of the characters who produce it. The writers effectively portray chefs, farmers, and cheesemakers as unlikely but appealing heroes by placing them as the protagonists in the familiar plot of comedy. In these stories, the local food producer encounters different types of challenges, usually placed in their way by the conventional agricultural system (factory farming, genetically modified plants, chemicals), and the system serves as the villain. Mayer suggests that such narratives fit within prototypical "resurrection" stories in which the protagonist suffers some setback, perseveres, and ends living happily ever after.[50] One appeal of such stories is that readers may quickly recognize the plot and characters, and anticipate how the story will conclude, but by casting unlikely actors (e.g., chefs and farmers) in the role of hero, creative genius, or entrepreneurial innovator, they add novelty to the stories.[51] Readers may get caught up in the story by the promise of a happy conclusion, by identifying with the hero, and by the detailed descriptions of the flavors, sights, and smells of kitchen, meadow, or seashore. The story connects readers to powerful emotions of hope and joy. Rooting for the protagonists aligns them on the side of the good, the true, and the right, while the sensual appeals to cooking, ripe produce, and amazing meals place them in an ideal food world where both culinary and social issues have happy resolutions.

Stories about local food, with their heroic characters, idyllic settings, and plots of overcoming adversity to achieve agricultural or culinary triumph, provide a "blueprint for how to think and act on the daunting environmental, moral, and health problems associated with our industrial food-system."[52] They do this in a variety of ways, most of which make emotional appeals and then suggest that following the call to act (i.e., to eat local foods) is the means to realize the positive emotions and minimize the guilt or shame attached to consumption of conventionally produced foods. Pioneer stories personalize those who produce local foods and make us want to support the farmer or innovative chef because their hard work, sacrifice, and creativity demand admiration.

These characters may inspire readers because they seem to embody the values about health, the environment, and taste that align with ours, and offer readers hope that local foods can change our unhealthy and uncaring food system. Memoirs provide a host of reasons to shop at farmers' markets and farm stands, follow a diet rich in local produce, and eat seasonally, and show that it is really quite easy. In short, narratives about local food are sense-making tools; they provide answers to questions about what local food is, why it is important, who produces it, why we should support them, and how to go about becoming locavores. Local food stories may help readers see how the production, distribution, and consumption of food are deeply moral endeavors. They may challenge or affirm their understanding of themselves as moral beings, and their communities as moral commonwealths. And they do this by yoking deep values and ideas—not just about food, but about community and the self, health and risk, and the morality of the market—to emotions. While emotions may not compel us to act, emotions such as guilt, anger, or love often predispose us to take actions that defend the self or others, or that challenge or conform to the existing social order.[53]

This extended discussion of the narratives and discourse surrounding local food is intended to highlight the underlying rationales and appeals that have propelled the local food movement, and it identifies the core ideas and values that may motivate involvement. The national discourse provides a ready-made set of understandings about justifications for entering and/or participating in the local food system. Although these are stories conveyed at the national level, they also are echoed in the discussions I have had with a wide variety of farmers and others involved in the central New York local food scene. The region's local producers are embedded in the stories and discourse about local food, and thus they may serve as sense-making tools that orient, motivate, or sustain their work.[54] Many producers, especially novices and chefs, spoke about reading Michael Pollan, learning about sustainability through environmental studies courses during college, or getting exposed to local food in culinary school. They rely on the various moral claims about local food as they sell their produce at farmers' markets, discuss the origin and mission of their farm on their CSA web page, or identify the sources of the foods on their menus.

I also tried to use this discussion of local food narratives to identify the ways in which morality and emotions have been harnessed to build interest and commitment among producers and consumers. The various types of food stories fall under the more general genre of "morality tales," in which the audience is confronted with the terrible outcomes (e.g., climate change, ill health, the breakdown of community) resulting from a series of deviations from the right pathway. Psychological anthropologists claim that morality tales direct and motivate action in two ways: first, by suggesting that an individual who follows or fails to follow some set of moral behaviors will suffer the same fate as the characters in the story; and second, by defining some values, goals, and actions as obligatory and thus as moral and others as wrong or immoral. Moreover, the motivational force from these kinds of accounts derives from the strong emotions attached to efforts to realize culturally approved goals (e.g., pride) or the failure to do so (e.g., shame).[55] Farrell argues that narratives are especially important because they are the foundation of any moral order: "Narratives structure moral orders, by which I mean that humans are believers embedded in stories big and small that separate sacred from profane and tell us who we are, why we are, what we are doing, and why it all matters. . . . Stories direct our lives and make what we do significant."[56] As will become apparent in the following chapters, my interviewees are embedded in several different stories about local food—sometimes showing how they embody particular roles, other times drawing on key ideas to explain how and why they are involved in the local food system.

Although the various narratives about local food paint a rosy picture in which it is prefigured as morally superior to the conventional food system, numerous scholars and journalists have identified the various ways that the moral vision has fallen short in practice. Some scholars argue that the promise of local food to re-embed farmers and consumers in more authentic communities based on trust, mutuality, and reciprocity in which the food itself is safer and more nutritious often fails for several reasons. First, neither party is actually committed to forming new communities, but instead instrumental concerns about price, profit, and consumer choice are prioritized.[57] Second, some populations are excluded from entry or full participation on the basis of race or class.[58] Another line of criticism points out how the goal of creating a more environmentally and socially just food system often remains unrealized as some local farmers may rely on non-sustainable practices such as the use of pesticides and chemical fertilizers or rely on exploitative labor practices.[59] Others raise a more fundamental critique of local food insofar as such systems are premised on the notion that we can build a food system that overcomes all of the ecological and social problems of the conventional food system simply through the "ethical" market choices of consumers. Individual choices do not easily aggregate into large-scale social change because food access, food security, food safety, and food equity are structural or systemic problems that require regulatory and policy changes.[60] In short, the moral motives and intentions at the heart of the local food movement and more broadly alternative food practices do not necessarily result in an objectively morally superior food system.

Yet the starting point of any effort to change the social world begins with the underlying moral vision of those who endeavor to transform the old or offer a new way of organizing the production and distribution of food. This book is a story about how a diverse set of farmers, chefs, artisanal food producers, and nonprofit organizations developed a moral vision and moral codes (or rules) that encouraged and sustained them on the road to developing a viable local market. I aim to show how the combination of several moral ideals—cooperation not competition; adherence to a contemporary pastoralism; a rejection of growth or profit as the primary goal; and a conception of the good life that emphasizes work-family balance, community formation, and a sense of wonder with the natural world—motivates entrance and sustains participation in the local food system.[61] More broadly, I am interested in what motivates farmers to grow food for the local market in central New York, and how they meet the start-up challenges and develop the market for local produce and meat within the constraints of their moral commitments, which may run counter to the rational pursuit of profit. Thus, the book is not a defense of local food but a report of how and why the actors involved in one such system made the decision to enter and build it. It is an effort to understand the constellations of values, beliefs, and moral principles that guide activity within an emerging agricultural market.

Sociologically, this book is an attempt to show how social action is informed, shaped, or directed by values, morality, and emotions. This may seem like an outdated endeavor, yet recent work to rehabilitate the role of values and to deepen our understanding of the important ways that emotions operate in social life suggest otherwise. In the next section of the chapter I discuss these literatures and describe the theoretical contribution I hope to make.

Morality, Emotions, and Action

Historically, values and morality played a central role in social theory and explanations of social action.[62] Although sociologists have tended to ignore or minimize the role of values, especially with the turn toward structural explanations, recently, a growing number of sociologists have reembraced values and morality as key components in their explanations of social action. A foundational starting assumption, in the words of sociologist Christian Smith, is that human beings are moral, believing animals, who "nearly universally live in social worlds that are thickly webbed with moral assumptions, beliefs, commitments, and obligations."[63] Similarly, Andrew Sayer argues that "the most important questions people tend to face in their everyday lives are normative ones of what is good or bad, what is happening, including how others are treating them, and of how to act, and what to do for the best."[64] He calls this "lay normativity" and contends that "moral understandings underpin all kinds of social interaction."[65] Yet social science tends to dismiss values and the ethical or moral dimensions of social life as unworthy of serious consideration. This is a serious oversight, Sayer contends, because it limits our ability to understand and explain social life: "Although this ethical dimension of life matters, enormously to us, social science is often poor at acknowledging and understanding it, preferring to account for action in terms of self-interest, or norm-following, or habitual action, or discursive constitution, which comprehensively fail to deal with the quality of ethical sensibilities."[66] Smith, Sayer, and others argue that the most important questions humans face as individuals and as members of collectivities are moral—how to act, how to minimize harm to self and others, how best to live, and how to create a world in which humans flourish and find meaning. If this assumption is true, then our research should aim to understand how morality informs and motivates action.

According to a number of different scholars, individuals are embedded in a moral order, which Justin Farrell defines as "an interpersonally and institutionally shared structure of moral beliefs, desires, feelings, and boundaries that are derived from narratives and rituals."[67] A moral order is the overarching meaning system that defines how humans ought to organize the social world, delimits the nature of mutual obligations and responsibilities we hold toward one another and the natural world, and tells us how to make the moral order real and binding. Geertz argues that a group's culture sets both its ethos ("the tone, character, and quality of their life, its moral and aesthetic style and mood; it is the underlying attitude towards themselves and their world") and its worldview ("their picture of the way things in sheer actuality are, their concept of nature, of self, of society"), and together, ethos and worldview provide the elements of the group's moral order. Ethos and worldview, according to Geertz, explain how the social world is organized and how it ought to be organized.[68]

As Farrell's definition suggests, institutional spheres are organized around specific moral orders and operate with their own moral codes. Within each sphere, individuals are encouraged to develop specific virtues, follow unique laws and norms to ensure order, and conform to institutionally defined boundaries that demarcate right and wrong actions and relationships. For example, economic sociologists argue that capitalistic markets encourage individuals to follow a variety of ethical virtues such as honesty, integrity, self-control, trustworthiness, and responsibility. The virtues demarcate social boundaries between good and bad market players, and should guide marketplace decisions and behaviors. Fourcade and Healy contend that markets are "explicitly moral projects, saturated with normativity," because they set out rules to limit behaviors such as cronyism that harm others and society as a whole, and rules to encourage pro-social actions.[69] We can think of a moral code as the set of values and rules that help individuals or groups to realize their vision of the moral order. Fine's study of amateur mushroom hunters illustrates the relationship between a moral order and its moral codes. The hunters adhere to one of three overarching ideologies about nature, and the moral codes or rules help them apply or adhere to the vision. For example, the "protectionist" vision of nature claims that "nature is a special realm—authentic and uncontaminated, fundamentally distinct from the built environment," and thus must be protected from human activities that will destroy it.[70] Protectionists follow the moral injunction to "foray softly," which is operationalized by such rules as walking in ways that do not damage soil and plants, collecting only mushrooms that are necessary for one's personal consumption or for identification purposes, and replacing the dirt in the hole after harvesting.[71]

Farrell also notes that individuals and groups are strongly motivated to "enact and sustain" their moral order, especially in the face of competition or challenges from others committed to a different moral order.[72] Within Western agriculture, two moral orders operate with different criteria for what constitute good, legitimate, and worthy agricultural practices and goals. On the one hand, conventional agriculture defines the good in terms of efficiency, rationality, market share, and profit maximization, and in turn, these values legitimate and encourage specific practices such as the use of chemical fertilizers or herbicides (because doing so may result in high crop yields in the short term). On the other, alternative agriculture (including local food systems) prioritizes non-economic concerns such as preserving biodiversity or relying on farming methods to reduce environmental damage. Farmers under this moral order organize their work so that these values are placed above profit. Weiler, Otero, and Wittman argue that action within alternative food networks is animated by a commitment to a moral economy that "involves production and exchange of goods and services on the basis of non-capitalist cultural norms of human goodness, fairness and economic justice."[73] These competing moral orders serve as the basic guide for farmers and others involved in the production and distribution of food, but they are guides that sometimes are followed and other times ignored. The key analytic puzzle is to identity how and why moral orders are activated.

The second assumption within this body of scholarship about values, morality, and social action is that moral beliefs and commitments influence human behavior and the ongoing organization of the social world. However, there is little consensus on how morality does this. Older sociological accounts about how deeply internalized moral norms and values dictate behavior have been soundly critiqued. Some have argued that accounts in which individuals attribute the cause of their behavior to deeply felt moral values and rules are simply post hoc justifications that serve to maintain the normative order of a situation. Ann Swidler, notably, has made a compelling case that values are a poor predictor of action because evidence of deep internalization often is weak as values and actions may not match.[74] Two individuals may hold the same values about the importance of purchasing locally produced food, for example, but both do not act on the values. For Swidler, values are important insofar as they are part of an individual's cultural tool kit. Our tool kit is comprised of a disparate set of ideologies, stories, and values that endow us with particular capacities to act, and we then deploy our tools to ensure that our behaviors fit specific institutional contexts or situations. The greater the fit between context and our "cultured capacities," the more likely we will be to engage in some behaviors and not others. Particular contexts offer opportunities and resources for some people to act on those values but deny them to others. If we return to our two people who both equally value local food, we may see different actions because one person lives in a food desert where local food is not available, while another lives next door to a weekly farmers' market. Swidler argues that we may best explain human action by looking at how individuals who are embedded within particular communities, contexts, and institutional settings develop repertoires of action from a cultural tool kit. Of course, the trick then, theoretically, is to understand what leads some to apply their tool kit and others to ignore or even disavow it and thus act in ways that deviate from their cultured capacities. Unfortunately, Swidler's account does not provide a lot of help answering this question. While she importantly directs our analytic attention to the contexts or institutions that tell us how to act and what goals we should seek to realize in our actions, she doesn't identify how individuals go about deciding when to use the tools in their tool kits and when not to do so. Moreover, she discounts the role that values and morality play in guiding action because they do not do so consistently and often they are invoked to help us justify our actions after the fact. Morality seems arbitrary at best, as humans will switch values as opportunities arise, or moral values themselves are secondary to finding an action that will best fit a given situation or context.[75]

Yet values and morality are important because they provide us with criteria we use to assess the legitimacy, desirability, and "rightness" of various courses of action. Fine and Sandstrom argue that we use shared understandings of "what is good, just, and proper" as sense-making tools that help us analyze, decide, and act as we make our way through daily life.[76] Similarly, Sayer argues that ethical dispositions "do not merely provide us with evaluations of what exists or has happened but orient our future actions." Moreover, he and others contend that we become committed to values such that they become deeply tied to our sense of self or character. When challenged or given an opportunity to act on those values, we often do so in order to preserve our commitments and identities.[77]

Pierre Bourdieu's concepts of the habitus and field are useful tools to explain how action and values or morality are related. The habitus is a system of durable and transposable dispositions that are inculcated through processes of socialization. It includes bodily phenomena such as posture and demeanor, cognitive schemas or frameworks to explain the world, and preferences in things such as art, music, and food. The habitus generates practices and perceptions that individuals apply consciously and unconsciously as they act in particular situations and settings or specific fields. Fields are institutional spaces consisting of a set of roles or social positions, rules to guide interaction and the exercise of power (such as the local food system or a religion), as well as setting out the goals or stakes of operating in the field.[78] The habitus provides individuals with a "feel for the game," or how to behave in a given field. According to Sayer, the habitus also includes ethical dispositions, which when activated in a particular field provoke "moral sentiments" (such as anger, shame, guilt, love). In turn, individuals use these moral sentiments to assess possible lines of action and then evaluate consequences of the chosen action; importantly, which ethical dispositions get activated vary by context.[79]

Combining Bourdieu's ideas about fields with Swidler's argument about the central role of contexts and institutional settings may help us gain a deeper understanding of how morality motivates action. In *Talk of Love*, Swidler notes that context is important because "some contexts systematize and unify culture, magnifying its influence. Culture's effects are strongest where the context demands and enforces public cultural coherence."[80] In other words, morality will motivate actions in contexts or institutional fields where members of a community share a set of moral values and codes and where members actively encourage conformity via rewards and penalties. This is evident in a variety of group settings such as religious organizations, restaurants, or corporate workplaces.[81] In addition, scholars who work within the framework of "convention theory" argue that institutions such as the family, the market, media, or the state are organized around a set of moral claims about identities, relationships, and practices that are more or less worthy and that individuals use to justify, support, and motivate actions.[82] Conventions are widely shared "systems of reciprocal expectations about the behavior of others, or more precisely as 'shared templates for interpreting situations and planning courses of action in mutually comprehensive ways that involve social accountability, . . . provid[ing] a basis for judging the appropriateness of action by self and others." The more deeply embedded individuals are in specific institutional fields, the more likely it is that they will be committed to the moral expectations and evaluative standards set by the conventions.[83] Many of the producers in the local food system are indeed deeply embedded in agricultural communities or relationships in which many of the core value commitments of alternative agriculture described earlier are understood to be the rules of the game, and they hold one another accountable to adhering to them.

More specifically, the contexts, or more broadly, the institutional settings (e.g., farmers' market or CSA) of local food may encourage individuals to adhere to the moral codes and the overarching moral order of alternative food in a number of ways. For example, farmers who are certified organic by the USDA are required to adhere to a set of practices regarding the use of chemicals or antibiotics. This in turn may encourage a moral commitment to producing safe and healthy food and following norms of honesty and transparency in the marketplace. Similarly, local producers who sell at farmers' markets may attempt to enforce rules about prices and food provenance in order to prevent the participation of vendors who sell food sourced from outside the region or state. Agricultural work itself is imbued with moral significance. Farmers and other producers regularly must make choices that can improve the safety of their work environment and the food they produce, and while many farming decisions about how to act are routinized, these acts are premised on some set of moral commitments.

In addition, the contexts in which farmers are embedded—agricultural markets, webs of family and friends and other farmers—provide norms about good farming practices and legitimate farm identities. Familial ties and producers' location within particular classed, educational, religious, and/or market settings shape their orientations toward food, eating, health, and the environment. The relationships engendered within these fields or settings provide a kind of moral education through which expectations and norms, identities and ways of being (i.e., the habitus) are nurtured, and to which they are held accountable.[84] For example, many farmers in the study who grew up in farming families or who had teen or young adult work experiences on farms follow some version of a widely shared ideology about the "good farmer" because parents and grandparents, teachers and farm bosses talk about it, and demonstrate the kinds of practices that define the virtues and moral characteristics attached to the role or identity. In general, the good farmer ideology suggests that such a person is a steward of land and livestock whose agricultural products should promote good health for consumers, whose practices should preserve the health of soil and land, crops, and animals, and who thus contributes to a just society. Stock concludes from their research that "good farming implies a moral and reflexive concern for the environment (both a farmer's personal land holdings and the environment as a shared whole), and an explicit concern for the health and well-being of their customers and people in general."[85] Such ideas and moral sentiments provide a "moral horizon that orients and motivates" by promising a meaningful life as well as present and future rewards, and help individuals construct a sense of the self.[86]

Scholars from across the social sciences generally agree that there is a strong relationship between the self and morality. Hoey argues that "identity and the moral are deeply intertwined in the unfolding narrative account of a person's life as a kind of quest to find a sense to that life."[87] Humans strive to cultivate some degree of certainty that they are moral beings, that others see them as moral, and that their actions and their sense of self are consistent. In addition, the more salient and central one's moral values, codes, and practices are to the sense of self, the more likely it is that one's actions will be motivated to realize those moral commitments.[88] Tavory makes the sociological point that we define ourselves by the kinds of actions (moral or otherwise) that we take and that we do so with the expectation that others will recognize us as moral beings and respond in ways that affirm our identities and actions.[89] He illustrates his claim with an example based on ethical consumption:

> What kind of mineral water, what eggs, and what meat one buys . . . become explicit self-definitional questions. If consumers buy "fair trade coffee," "freedom eggs," or "free-ranging beef" they are suddenly offered another horizon for their actions, as it defines them as certain kind of people—both politically and ecologically. . . . Ethical consumerism is an attempt to imbue an action that is usually not experienced as self-defining with an explicit inter-situational position, to transform it into an act that can perhaps be termed "self-signaling."[90]

Tavory continues by noting that when we act to present ourselves as moral beings, it elicits emotional responses from our self and those with whom we interact. This idea can be traced back to micro-sociological traditions (e.g., Charles Horton Cooley's "looking-glass self" is a key concept). We assess what kind of person we are based on the kinds of emotions that arise during interaction (both in real time and in our imaginations). The emotions we and others experience are cues that signal how closely our actions match the moral demands of a given situation and how closely action and identity match; we feel pride or joy when actions fit our conception of our moral self but shame, guilt, or embarrassment when our actions fall short of the moral standards we hold or that are endorsed by our community.[91] Sayer notes that "sentiments such as pride, shame, envy, resentment, compassion and contempt are not just forms of 'affect' but are evaluative judgments of how people are being treated in regards to what they value, that is things they consider to affect their well-being."[92] Thus, emotions act as cues that direct our attention to our actions, which in turn "frame our decision-making," help us identify and order possible lines of action, and also push us to adjust our behaviors to keep them in line with our moral values and sense of a moral self.[93]

Randall Collins contends that we experience the core primary emotions (anger, fear, happiness, sadness) either during interaction with others or during particular situations (e.g., harvesting one's crop), and they generate "emotional energy." These energies, in turn, may generate long-lasting moods that orient individuals toward lines of action, support views of the self, and promote moral sentiments (i.e., "feelings of what is right and wrong, moral and immoral").[94] Moral sentiments are more durable and more closely tied to individuals' sense of self than short-lived "reflex" emotions such as anger, fear, or surprise, and thus may be more likely to serve as guides for action. In turn, individuals are likely to think about the actions guided by their moral sentiments and examine those actions as individuals assess how well they reinforce their fundamental identity as a moral being.[95]

At the same time, emotions and moral sentiments do not reside only in the individual. They also may be connected to broader ethics that individuals and communities use to guide behavior and address social problems. For example, in an "ethic of community an action is deemed wrong because a person fails to carry out her duties within a community, or to the social hierarchy within a community," and such action may elicit contempt and guilt.[96] In short, powerful emotions may compel us to act on particular moral values in order to feel that we are acceptable to ourselves as well as to members of our community.

Scholarship on morality and social action provides a set of explanatory concepts that will guide my analysis of how the local food system in central New York operates. To summarize: individuals enter the local food system with a set of moral values—some of which are specific to food and agriculture such as animal husbandry and some more general about health and risk. These ethical dispositions and moral worldviews are shaped by their embeddedness in communities of discourse and practice and from both, individuals develop a moral identity. Specific local food contexts (e.g., farmers' markets or dealing with a stubborn field of weeds) cue or activate an individual's moral commitments. These in turn influence decision and actions. Finally, as individuals assess their actions, they elicit emotions that confirm their moral self and worldview or cause them to alter their actions to bring them back in line with that moral sense.

Nature of the Study

The project originated in 2018, when I started collecting data for a study of the local food system in four of the eight central New York counties. This research sought to understand how the local food system emerged and developed during the past decade. I aimed to include a wide range of actors involved in local food production: small farmers and CSAs, meat and poultry farmers, farm-to-table restaurants, cheesemakers, foragers, farmers' markets, and agricultural nonprofit organizations. In the end, I conducted interviews with fifty-one individuals who represent forty-five different farms or organizations. These include seven CSAs, seven meat producers, four cheesemakers, seven small farms that produce for farmers' markets, their own farm stands, or institutional buyers, four local food retailers, six self-identified locavore restaurants, seven individuals who work on food issues for local governments (e.g., farmers' market managers) or agricultural nonprofit organizations, two farmstead breweries, and one owner of a small farm distribution co-op (see the appendix for a list of participants). This set of participants represents nearly 40 percent of all actors involved with the local food system in the targeted counties. All were white, and most had a college education and were from the middle class, albeit from the lower end economically.[97] The majority of producers were fully employed on their farms, restaurants, or retail nonprofit jobs, but five had off-farm jobs and two entered the local food system after retirement. The CSAs ranged in size from thirty subscribers to three hundred, and most farmed on two to twelve acres. Meat producers ran herds of beef cattle from 40 to 150 and some had as many as 80 hogs and 50 lambs (although only two had 150 head of cattle). Most of the labor on the participating farms came from the farmers and their family members, and then short-term seasonal help from high school or college students. I conducted face-to-face interviews of forty-five to ninety minutes with the majority of participants, but conducted a handful of interviews via phone and Zoom during the first year of the pandemic.

As I began to read and code my interview transcripts, I came to see how each of my interviewees became involved with local food and how they persevered through the challenges of producing food in a less than hospitable market and climate. Their comments about working toward sustainable agriculture or serving as good stewards of the land, as well as the ways in which they spoke so passionately about the joys of farming and the pride they felt in what they produced, led me to focus the book around the ways in which morality and emotions shape the decisions that guided their entry into and continued participation in the local food system. In chapters 2 and 3 I draw heavily on the responses of my interviewees and do so more often than may be common in books that rely on qualitative data. This is a choice to allow the voices of farmers, chefs, and others involved in the local food system to be heard directly because they are among the invisible workers to provide essential services to the public. Many also engage in "dirty work" that tends to render them invisible and of lower status. Sociologists define dirty work as paid labor that "may be simply physically disgusting. It may be a symbol of degradation, something that wounds one's dignity. Finally, it may be dirty work in that it in some way goes counter to the more heroic of our moral conceptions."[98] Not only are those who work literally in dirt, manure, or chicken guts often stigmatized, but they are not considered moral actors by the rest of society. Yet in their voices we will hear the ways in which they consider their work to be fundamentally moral and themselves to be morally worthy individuals. In keeping with my research ethics protocol, all individuals, farms, restaurants, and organizations have been given a pseudonym.

Plan of the Book

Chapter 2: The Moral Foundations of Local Food Production

In this chapter, I identify the various moral codes about local food that motivate farmers and chefs to enter into the local food system and the ways in which these codes sustain their participation. I show how following their moral commitments about agriculture and hospitality engenders powerful emotions that affirm their identities as farmers and chefs and reinforces their sense that involvement in the local food system is good. In particular, I discuss how producers' embeddedness in specific communities, practices, and sets of meaning about food help them create the moral order of local food. I illustrate how different types of producers construct unique moral orders about food based on their mission (e.g., selling meals at a restaurant versus growing organic vegetables), training, and base of consumers.

Chapter 3: Building the Local Foodshed

Uncertainty and risk are endemic to agricultural life and are exacerbated for local food producers as they struggle to create new markets that can compete with conventional agricultural markets. This chapter focuses on the practical challenges associated with local food production, which itself is imbued with moral imperatives. I show how producers struggle to balance moral commitments and profit, overcome the fickleness of consumers and institutional buyers, and cope with the limited infrastructure that supports local food in central New York. They do this, I argue, by developing a market based on an alternative set of norms that prioritize non-economic values, goals, and relationships over economic ones. In effect, they attempt to create a moral market and an economy of regard in order to differentiate local food from conventionally produced food and make the market more reliable and stable because participants are bound together by a shared commitment to a moral vision of agriculture.

Chapter 4: Morality, Emotions, and the Future of Local Food

I begin the final chapter with a discussion of how the COVID-19 pandemic affected local farmers and report on my interviewees' assessments about the future of local food. The global pandemic created severe financial challenges for local food producers, as well as new opportunities. The popular media have identified a deep-seated fragility to the American food system that runs from California's vegetable fields to the meatpacking plants in the Great Plains to the supermarkets and restaurants in most cities. The pandemic threatened, and in some cases has toppled, the food system like a row of dominos due to bottlenecks in the distribution system and shutdowns of various industries. At the same time, the press has reported on a surge of interest in local foods, with CSAs unable to meet the demand. In this chapter, I discuss how the local food system in central New York responded in creative ways to the crisis and what that response may promise for the continued viability of local food in the region. I then return to sociological questions about the nature and drivers of human action. I make the case that our explanations for when, how, and why people engage in some courses of action and not others may be more complete if we reincorporate values and emotions into these explanations. I discuss how focusing on the interplay of emotions, production, and morality helps us understand the kinds of behaviors that may not seem rational or financially rewarding. In particular I explore the key finding that the emotions producers experience during the course of producing and marketing their goods serve as cues they use to assess the "rightness" of their activities and moral codes. This evaluation process may reinforce production practices and identities and/or trigger changes to both. This approach runs counter to much of the literature about human action that stresses the routine and even subconscious nature of most action. However, given the consequential nature of farming and food production, I argue, farmers more often must reflect on their actions in order to minimize the potential to harm those who eat the food they produce.

2

The Moral Foundations of Local Food Production

I began my interview with Liam Cook, owner of Harmony Farm, with a tour. He showed me the neat fifteen-by-fifty-foot plots on which he grew various types of vegetables as he explained how they are separated by family (cruciferous vegetables in one plot, alliums in another) in order to maximize soil and plant health, along with the rows of blueberry bushes, the greenhouse, and the future site of a chicken coop. He spoke passionately about the necessity of rotating crops and letting plots lie fallow in order to keep the soil healthy. After the tour we sat down in the chilly loft of his barn over cups of tea and he told me the story of the farm. His initial interest in farming came in the early 1990s, after reading Rachel Carson's *Silent Spring*, which sensitized him to the dangers of industrial agriculture and awakened in him a passion to grow his own food. It would take another fifteen years before the farm became a reality. He moved back to New York from California and purchased forty-five acres that had been owned by a member of his extended family but never farmed. This makes Liam a "greenhorn" who has learned to farm largely by trial and error.[1]

He began small and tried selling at farmers' markets, but sales were slow; he would return from a Saturday market with too much unsold produce and it would just go to waste. However, he cultivated relationships with a number of area CSA farmers who took him under their wing, and within a year he had started his own CSA. Given the size of his land and the growing demand for local food in the region, I asked whether he planned on making the farm larger or expanding the number of subscribers. His answer, that he was deliberately opting to stay small, I discovered, would be echoed by his peers in subsequent interviews, and it revealed some of the core values that motivate him to grow local food:

At thirty subscribers I mostly break even. I mean, in fifteen years of doing this, Steve, I think I've made a profit of any note once. And I just happened not to have so many expenses that year. I had enough seed, I had enough fertilizer, I didn't have to put tires on the tractor, the truck didn't need major work. . . . I'm not driven by profit. I'm not trying to make money. But I need to break even. And I always had lots of angst about raising my prices. But why did I keep doing it? I could ask myself that question and it keeps coming back to I want to grow my own food. And since I'm able to grow this much on this piece of, this parcel of land, what am I going to do with it? And I want to be diversified. And whether it's my little tiny two-and-a-half-acre CSA, or a five-thousand-acre farm in California, diversity is key. It's required for a healthy system. And we certainly don't do that. Our culture has it all wrong. All of it. Just from the beginning, with all the assumptions and all of our values and all of our mores, which are based in competition and resource extraction for the good of humans at the expense of all other life forms. It's just, we're so backwards. We're so destructive. It's mind-boggling to me and it keeps getting worse. So I'm out here on forty-five acres saying I'm not going to do that. And so, if I'm a reluctant capitalist that's fine, but I'd rather not be a capitalist at all. And none of us should be. Capitalism is based on competition and stepping on everybody who's in your way.

Liam voiced a countercultural perspective about growth, competition, and profit. He spoke at length about his duty to be a good steward of the land, to make his farm sustainable and self-sufficient. To this end, he had started beekeeping to promote pollination, and hoped to add a brood of chickens to serve as his source of manure. His discussion of these new additions to the farm were couched in his critique of industrial agriculture. I asked him whether he added bees in order to produce honey as a valued-added product for the farm to bolster his income, which is a common practice among the area's producers. He scoffed at my question:

Look. I have 180 blueberry bushes and apple trees and I need pollinators. I've rented hives in the past and that's when I have my best crops. But why rely on someone else's bees? I've tried to learn from the local people, and the local people all seem to be hooked into the industrial mindset of beekeeping. . . . So I've got the Langstroth hives, which are square boxes, and this is not a natural situation for the bee colony. It makes it easy for humans to extract the honey, and the mindset is to have the bees produce honey all through the spring, summer, and fall, and then take it and feed them sugar water over the winter. And that's—how can you not understand that that's got to be part and parcel of the colony collapse disorder issue? And you have weak bees who aren't being fed their normal diet. You know, it's like feeding cows corn. They don't eat corn in the wild. . . . So I took a workshop for organic beekeeping down in the Hudson Valley, and what they said is, "It's so obvious, so simple and so right." You leave the honey for the bees over winter. If there's something left in the spring you can have it. And if you need to feed them, feed them a mixture of honey, chamomile tea, and water. But the industrial mindset is I've got to get what I can get. It's like the guys who tap maple trees and put a vacuum on it. What, the maple tree is not giving it up fast enough for you? You've got to suck it out? So you're getting an idea of where I lie in the world.

Despite early mistakes, weathering the usual difficulties posed by pests, weather, and weeds, and the challenges associated with his ecological commitment to minimize fossil fuels and chemicals (nearly everything is done by hand on the farm), Liam remained enthusiastic about his vocation. His enthusiasm stemmed in part from his desire to grow healthy, fresh food for members of his community that will be a true alternative to that offered at the local Walmart, in part to build a community of like-minded souls who want to live deeply rooted to the land, and in part to follow and promote an ethic of care that he believes has largely vanished in America. Increasingly he wants the farm to serve the dietary needs of more than his middle-class subscribers, and thus he donates extra produce to a local food pantry and has leased some of the land to a group of inner-city residents so they can grow their own food.

He noted, toward the end of the interview, that he found farming to be among the most rewarding things he has ever done: "Farming is work. Farming is physical labor. It's beautiful physical labor. You are in contact with the land. It keeps you sane. It keeps you grounded. It keeps you understanding the value of nature. But we're so disenfranchised. We're so disassociated from that." This statement identifies how the sensory experiences of farming cue both strong emotions and the values that undergird his decision to enter the local food system.

My conversation with the owner of Harmony Farm reveals the ways in which his work as a farmer is shaped by a moral vision about market economies and the social world, agriculture, and the environment. It is evident in his concerns about how the pursuit of profit above all else in conventional agriculture, even local agriculture, harms the natural and human worlds; in his lament about the loss of biodiversity and despoliation of the farmland by pesticides and herbicides; and in his goal to grow healthy food that will not just nourish bodies but engender community. Liam Cook's moral vision also is shaped and reinforced by his relationship with fellow CSA farmers, his exposure to organic farming workshops and literature, and the emotional feedback he receives from the acts of sowing and reaping.

In this chapter I take up questions about why individuals enter an occupation that is physically demanding and financially precarious. What motivates them to enter the field and what keeps them in it despite the myriad challenges they face? To what extent is farming and other work within the local food economy understood as a moral calling? In particular, I look at how particular social contexts and life experiences shape individuals' moral codes and then how those codes pull them into local food production. I then show how the cultivation of support networks and specific kinds of interactions they experience in the field or kitchen deepens their moral calling and sustains them.

The Good Farmer

"There's very, very few people who can make a lot of money off of farming. And there are a few, you know. There are sorta these organic grower/sustainable farming rock-star-type guys and they'll tell you all about how they are grossing $350,000 from two acres. And maybe they are, but they've got ideal markets like Westchester County or Manhattan or the suburbs of Chicago, but it's not here." This wry comment from Keith Stevens, owner of Red Maple CSA, sums up the economic hopes of small farmers in central New York and raises the question of what motivates him and others to this kind of work when the economic benefits seem limited and elusive. While economic motives play an important role, as do such factors as the nature of the available agricultural markets, size of farm and growing conditions, and membership in communities of farming practice, they are tempered by the operative understanding of the nature and purpose of food production to which farmers subscribe. Some scholars have found clear attitudinal and value differences between conventional and alternative farmers, and discuss how these beliefs and values drive decisions to enter farming and what practices they use (e.g., monoculture versus mixed crops, pesticide and herbicide use).[2] Research about the "good farmer" (introduced in the previous chapter) highlights how farmers and ranchers understand their work as moral. Good farming is anchored in a set of values, practices, and identities that at the collective level stress stewardship and sustainability, community and relationships; and at the individual level stress such virtues as self-reliance, honesty, industriousness, and hard work.

Stewardship is an overarching ethic that encompasses imperatives to conserve resources, build or preserve the fertility of the soil and/or the health of animals, and protect the natural environment. At its most basic level, stewardship involves the use of the natural world to promote human flourishing, but with an awareness of the constraints imposed by particular ecological systems. A more environmentally conscious or green farming ethic stresses sustainability—that is, the use of food production and distribution methods that ensure the ability to feed the human population by farming in ways that soil, water, and seed are not depleted in the long term, and that also ensure the ongoing vitality of human communities. The good farmer who follows the goals of sustainability is one who uses "methods that maintain fertile soils and viable crops in perpetuity."[3] In his book profiling roughly forty Minnesota farmers, Gary Holthaus captures the green ethic side of the good farmer identity, and the contrast between the visions of alternative and conventional agriculture in his chapter about Peggy Thomas: "Maximizing crop and animal production was never an aim. We always wanted to respect the animals, take care of the whole environment—create a diverse, natural production. We're not simply trying to farm in the conventional way, but to manage the whole place towards biodiversity. Sustainability means that you can live on the land, live with the land, forever."[4]

Environmental historian Donald Worster contends that good farming, more broadly, "makes people healthier, promotes a just society and preserves the earth and its network of life."[5] The literature about local food production, as well as the larger body of scholarship on alternative agriculture, builds on the notion of the good farmer. For example, Bruce notes how farmers who are new to the profession often claim that they switched careers in order to reform an industrial food system that fails to provide safe and healthy food for consumers and despoils the land. Similarly, Beingessner and Fletcher's research on Canadian local farmers shows that they are champions for production methods that limit chemical pesticide and herbicide use, aim to greatly reduce dependency on fossil fuel, and promote biodiversity. They, like other scholars, also find that local food producers share a second set of values that may set them apart from conventional producers, placing honesty, transparency, and relationality over maximizing yield and profit.[6] That's not to say that the farmers and others I interviewed were not interested in making money, only that other moral concerns acted as counterweights to purely economic goals. Some farmers, especially some of the new farmers, had the financial resources (due to family financial backing or off-farm or retirement income) that allowed them to minimize the profit motive, while others were driven by strong anticapitalist commitments.

Another focus of the good farmer ethic is a concern to serve those who live in their community and/or to build a community dedicated to the same values that animate their vision of alternative agriculture. Research about CSAs and farmers' markets suggests that building community is a challenging task, yet it continues to motivate some farmers to enter a local food system. Thompson summarizes this ideal when he writes, "A local food system embeds people in practices whereby their commerce with nature and with one another creates an enduring sense of place. In a local food system, even people who buy (rather than grow) most of their food at farmers' markets or through cooperative arrangements encounter the same people repeatedly, week after week. They build bonds with them, and honesty and mutual respect."[7] In his study of organic farmers in the Midwest, rural sociologist Paul Stock argues that ultimately good farming is moral because it entails providing care for not just the land but for the families and communities who rely on what the land produces.[8]

Concerns about values that should guide interaction and shape the relationships within the local food system speak to the individual motivations of good farming. Those who work in this field often feel called to this kind of work as a way of realizing an ideal self. The role of the good farmer requires one to ask, What kind of person am I, or do I hope to be? Good farmers see themselves as individuals who care deeply about others and the natural world, and care deeply about the health and welfare of those who consume their food. When morality is central to their sense of self, individuals may then feel a greater obligation to act on or live out those core values, and the literature about local food producers suggests that their moral identities drive their actions. For example, Weber, Heinze, and DeSoucey uncovered not just the environmental values that motivate entry into alternative agriculture, but also values about authentic relationships and the authentic self. They argue that these producers deeply hold to the values of transparency, connectedness, sincerity, and honesty, which they categorize as a commitment to authenticity. In their interviews with ranchers, they repeatedly heard that their commitment to grass-fed beef was not just a commercial enterprise but an expression of the ranchers' fundamental moral identity and that "they obtained emotional energy from connecting their work to their sense of self and the moral values represented in the [larger] movement."[9]

In short, much of the research about local food production suggests that it rests on a distinct moral foundation, which motivates entry and sustains participation. Farming is a moral vocation to the degree that "the primary motivation and objective of the job arise from and affirm collectively agreed upon understandings of the good, the true, the just, and/or serve the interests of the public . . . or a world in need."[10] Yet human motivations for action are complex, and often we are unaware of precisely why we set off on one course of action over another. Action rarely simply follows from our values, but that doesn't mean that values are unimportant. In the next section, I set out the argument that local food producers follow particular moral codes, albeit imperfectly and incompletely. Their codes serve as touchstones; values and moral codes work synergistically with experiences, contexts, and one's sense of self to guide action. Moreover, as producers enact the role of the good farmer in their work of sowing, reaping, or cooking, their very actions are assessed in light of this ideal and either are affirmed or become a cause to reassess their code, their work, and their self-worth. As Barnard argues in his study of freegan dumpster divers, "Moral beliefs and identities are not just prior to moral action but are constructed in a dialectical fashion through action, creating a sense of one's moral place" in the social world.[11] In the rest of the chapter, I examine what motivates farmers, cheesemakers, and chefs to enter the local food system in central New York and/or why they participate in this system. In particular, I pay attention to how producers' moral codes influence entry and participation, and how moral concerns are balanced by market or economic concerns. I also discuss how their experiences of farming create an emotional feedback loop that often serves to motivate entry or confirms the rightness of their choice to produce food for the local market.

The Moral Codes of the Field

There are multiple pathways into local food production among the twenty-six farmers and cheesemakers in the study. How they entered the field and what values guide their involvement depend on three factors: first, their status (newcomers, returners [those who grew up on a farm, left for a different career but then returned to farming], and legacy farmers [those who grew up on the farm they work now]); second, their particular educational and life experiences that push or pull them into farming; and third, their ability to recognize and seize opportunities. Although there is no single moral code that shapes entry and participation into the local food system, all farmers identified a broad set of environmental and communal values that motivated entry and led them to adopt an ethic of care. The differences between the three types is a matter of emphasis, with the new farmers focusing more on sustainability and reforming the food system, while returnees and legacy farmers are more likely to stress husbandry or stewardship on the one hand and the family on the other.

New Farmers: Sustainability and the Enchantment of Farming

Eleven producers have no background in farming and came to it following college or as a second career. Among them, there are four CSAs, one farmer-turned-baker, one cheesemaker, two meat producers, and three growers of specialty crops such as microgreens, asparagus, and mushrooms. Several of the CSA and meat farmers began their careers during or within five years after college, while the other newcomers came to farming as a second or supplemental career. One of the striking features of their stories about how they came to farming is the ways in which the pathways involve the merger of core values and emotional experiences of working the land. Experiences and values work synergistically to motivate entry and sustain involvement in local food production. In other words, the sensory experiences of farming give rise to joy and a sense that farming allows one to live authentically. These emotions and experiences then both confirm and shape the values that guide their work.

The younger new farmers reported powerful "aha" or conversion-type experiences in which they had a sense of finding themselves or a home in the world by farming. For some, farming quickly became a more joyful, rewarding vocation than anything else they could imagine or had experienced. For example, Melissa Harrison, owner of Hidden Hills Farm, spoke about the deadening effect of her post-college office job. Sitting in front of a computer hour after hour, week after week, made her realize that she needed to be active and doing something tangible. She started gardening at home, and a friend suggested she try farming. The thought was incredible to her: "The first time I heard someone say that I thought they said to me, Why don't you become a bus driver? Why don't you become a janitor? Like, that's what it sounded like to me when they said try farming." A year later, another friend alerted her to a one-year residency at a farm in Massachusetts. She decided to give it a try, and the initial experience proved to be magical and transformative:

> From day one, honestly, it blew my mind to be in this world of the senses. So the ducks are running by and quacking and you go out and you pick up your egg and you come in and eat it. You milk the cow. You are touching, you are smelling, you are under the sky. And these things blew my mind. I couldn't believe that this could be my life, to be in these elements. And so, I would say that's the second part of the two biggest motivations for me.

At the same time, farming appealed to her because it articulated with values and ideals she possessed from her religious upbringing and some of the courses she took in college. In particular, her social science courses helped her identity the fundamental problems of capitalism that ran counter to her convictions of what is right: "The fact that the economy is founded on exploitation and requires slavery and war . . . and feeling this horribleness within me that I'm participating in it. So, I was looking for ways that I myself could step out of participation in such a destructive machine that is our culture, that is our economy." After two years of working apprenticeships, she returned to New York and started a very small CSA on land her family helped her find. Melissa's account shows how values and particular experiences, as well as the search for a vocation that would allow her to be true to her sense of self, worked together to push her toward farming.

Two other CSA farmers spoke about young adult farming jobs that made them feel called to this life. Keith Stevens recalled how his first internship at a dairy and cheesemaking venture awakened in him the desire to make farming his life's work: "That was my first exposure to real, like okay, get up at 5:00 a.m. in the morning and work till 8:00 at night farming lifestyle. And it just hit home and I just really enjoyed it." Subsequent jobs in organic farms and orchards cemented the "rightness" of that first job. When I asked him what made running the CSA rewarding, his reply echoed that of Melissa Harrison:

> I think for me the satisfaction is definitely just being outside, hands in the soil. Those basic things are super important to me for whatever reason—my physiology or whatever. I've got to have that. Farming somehow has just hit the mark in terms of the kind of work that I like to do physically and emotionally, and I think it's the sun and the soil, being part of that for a substantial amount of every day for a number of months of the year is really important to me.

Paul Weber, owner of Stillwater Farm, also worked on farms during and after college, and like Keith, he also fell in love with farming immediately. After college he worked for a CSA that exposed him to all aspects of farming—from working with draft and dairy animals to learning how to grow a wide variety of fruits, vegetables, and grains. His own farm was modeled after this whole-diet, year-round CSA. Early during our interview I learned of the struggles in his early years with making his CSA economically viable. When I asked why he kept on, he broke into a big smile: "I just like working on this farm. I love being outside. I like working with animals." He continued by talking about the autonomy of his job and the everyday challenges and variability that come with farming, but then he turned back to his college education and how it deeply shaped his identity and values:

> I was a philosophy student at college, and I was very much into ethics and morality, and so I thought a lot about what is a good life, what as a human being should I be doing with my time. And I think farming is necessary. I have to eat and if I'm going to do something with my time I may as well do something that's necessary. And I remember reading *Omnivore's Dilemma* when I was a senior in college. And I haven't read it again since then but I just remember, and you've read it, that last section where he's talking about the hunting and gathering, I think it was in that section where he was talking about how brutal hunting is in a way. But he [Pollan] said that he, in that experience he saw the beauty and the necessity of it. And that to me is what I love about farming on a really deep level. Like, I have to eat. If I can spend my time growing that food, that's awesome. . . . I love it because it feels like I can be doing something that's really meaningful and necessary and it's now providing me with the time and the financial ability to do the other things that I really love. I just love it. I say to my wife all the time, "I can't imagine at this point doing anything else." I certainly couldn't imagine working for anybody else. And I am really hard pressed to think of anything that I think I would like as much as this.

In his account, Paul touches on the elements of the greenhorn entry story: farming experiences give rise to powerful, positive emotions that dovetail with an emergent set of ecological values from his college education, and together they give him a sense of doing something inherently good and coming to realize an authentic moral self.

Not all of the new farmers had such transformative experiences, but most gave voice to the wonder of the field. For example, a part-time mushroom grower likened working on his crop to "therapy." Ed Peters, who married into a family farm (Lucky Acres) and now runs the family meat business while teaching full-time, recalled how the first time he ate the farm's lamb he became hooked: "After I ate the meat once I said, 'Oh my God, this is the best lamb I ever had.' And it changed everything." He continued by contrasting his work as a teacher to his work as a farmer, and while the former is still important and meaningful, farming offers him one way to be fully human: "This is immediate. What I do here on the farm, it's tangible. I can touch it. I can sell it. You can see it. It's so different than what we do in the classroom. This is all physical. That's all mental." In this comment he echoes the perspective of Liam Cook insofar as farming offers a remedy for alienation.

In the voices of these farmers we hear the ways in which agricultural work has enchanted them, and how that enchantment cemented a commitment to local food production. In their work about CSA subscribers and farmers, Thompson and Coskuner-Balli found that participating in local food production fostered emotional connections to the land, narrowed the separation of mind and body, enhanced the importance of embodied knowledge, and most commonly led to experiences of surprise, awe, and wonder while tilling, weeding, or harvesting.[12] As evinced in their comments, enchantment happens as the actual work of farming in the outdoor setting seems to trigger strong positive emotions. Scholars who study emotions and rituals—and farming tasks may take on the character of a ritual—suggest that emotions serve as clues about how to interpret what's going on and who we are, and how to assess whether our behavior is correct and whether it aligns with our sense of self.[13] Positive emotions, such as joy or pride, reinforce one's sense that one is a good farmer and that one is engaged in the right kind of behavior. This emotional attunement may be heightened the more often an individual experiences the connection between specific behaviors and positive emotions, which in turn may engender more durable moods. For example, Keith Stevens and I were talking about the joys and challenges of farming, and I shared my own satisfaction and happiness watching my small plots of carrots, beans, and tomatoes grow. Keith replied, "Yes, it eggs you on. You see it growing. Then weed it, and things are getting better and better and better. You see the improvements you can make as you go." The act of farming produces positive emotions that encourage him to continue in his vocation and more importantly show him how his actions and senses shape and reinforce his understanding of his work and identity as fundamentally moral. In other words, the experiences of tending the garden, growing healthy food in healthy soil, help farmers develop a moral self.[14]

The connections among emotions, values, and action also were evident in producers' discussions of their core ecological motives. Nearly every interviewee identified some set of environmental concerns that drove them into farming or affected how they farm. Local food environmentalism ranged from fairly simple understandings that the role of farmer entailed a duty to safeguard the health of soil, crop, or animal life to more elaborate critiques of conventional agriculture (as intimated in the opening vignette about Liam Cook), and a felt duty to produce in ways that would ensure sustainability, promote biodiversity, and yield safe and healthy food. New farmers were more likely to hold or follow a more elaborate environmental ethic or to make it a higher priority than other types of producers.

Melissa Harrison repeatedly spoke about the environmental values that motivate her work. Initially this topic came up as we spoke about her declining participation in the region's farmers' markets:

> SE: And I think I recall you saying that people only want perfect vegetables and not every vegetable is perfect.

MH: That's really annoying, yeah. And that actually is a huge—I would say—I would venture, without having numbers in front of me, more pesticides are used for aesthetic perfection than for any other reason. And so, we are poisoning our earth. We are the earth. All the creatures are being poisoned because of this illogical need for perfection.

As our conversation progressed, she talked about her development as an organic farmer and the move to embrace a naturalistic or biologically driven process to manage weeds and pests, rather than rely on chemicals:

There's an advancing eco-agriculture, which is a new group we're more into recently, as far as growing information. And they focus on soil health and plant health. Whereas NOFA [Northeast Organic Farming Association] has kind of gone much more Cornell's [University] route, which is toward organic sprays. It's like the twin of chemical agriculture but it's organic. Instead of focusing on how do we feed the plants and make them healthy, it's like someone who's into natural medicine but all they do is take supplements instead of eating healthy. . . . We don't spray for pests, even organic sprays. So we're much more geared toward this advancing eco-agriculture, which focuses on soil health and plant nutrition as a way to ward off pests.

Keith Stevens made his commitment to sustainability even more explicit during our interview and on the farm's web page. The latter begins with this announcement:

My farming practice focuses on soil health. To work a small plot of land year and after year requires a lot of attention to fertility, soil tilth, and erosion control. . . . [I] use crop rotations, natural compost, and nitrogen-fixing cover crops to maintain high soil fertility even while maintaining high intensity farming [rather than fossil fuel-based soil amendments]. In a nutshell, that is the dividing line between organic and conventional agriculture.

When I asked him why he grows for local food markets, he offered a classic defense of local food, centered around the goal of limiting the miles food must travel in order to ameliorate climate change.[15] While Keith may not have read Kingsolver or McKibben, his explanation about why he grows local food mirrors the kinds of moral claims in the popular discourse discussed in chapter 1:

> I think it's just a way to live out some sustainability perspectives that I have and that I think obviously are shared among a lot of people. A growing perspective that food miles are part of the problem with a culture that's overly reliant on fossil fuels, and that that could be a danger in the long term, that if we're going to hit a point where there's a crunch on fossil fuel supplies it may just be sort of a house of cards, you know, that we're stacking so much reliance of our food system on a fossil fuel-based approach with lots and lots of food miles built in to every calorie we consume, that someday that's going to come back and bite us. So at least let's pioneer a way, see if it's possible to grow some of this stuff locally.

Although Ed Peters of Lucky Acres Farm did not offer as full-throated a commitment to sustainability as other new farmers, he spoke about the importance of honoring the lives of his sheep and cattle by making sure that every edible part is used. He aims to produce meat for nose-to-tail eaters:

> I remember my grandparents were so poor they would get a leg of lamb and they literally would spend all day Sunday cutting it—I mean when it was done you saw the bone. There was nothing left. They used every part of the animal. If they had a live animal, like if they got a live lamb, they would make tripe with the intestines, they'd cook the liver, and all that.... When I process my animals, nobody wants that. Nobody wants

the tongue, no one wants the liver, the heart. But I keep all that because I can't justify that going to waste. And I have people who feed it to their dogs and I do have some people who want it. So I give it to them. I don't want any money for it. I just don't want it to go to waste. You know? And to me that's all about the footprint that we're leaving here. And that animal did give its life for us, so I want to make sure that we utilize as much of that animal as possible.

In this comment he articulates a zero-waste approach to food and tacitly invokes an ethical orientation to farming in which future generations will not be harmed.

While most of the new farmers were motivated to enter the local food system by moral concerns about sustainability, care for the earth, and the safety of the food supply, a few of the new farmers stumbled into local food, and their ecological commitments developed along the way. These were the second-career farmers who saw opportunities either in the local food market or with the land they owned/purchased. For example, one couple bought an old farm, just under forty acres, right before they were to be married. With little extra cash and her strong desire not to live with his parents, they turned the barn into an apartment and started to grow their own food, which included chickens and a few beef cattle that could graze on their pastures. These accidental homesteaders turned out to be very good farmers, and when they realized that they could not eat all the beef or chicken or eggs, they decided to start selling to their neighbors and then at one of the farmers' markets. Thus, Twin Ponds Farm was founded. Sarah and Tom Wilson learned how to raise and market grass-fed beef through a process of trial and error, talking with veteran farmers, and attending conferences about organic agriculture and farm management. Although they started as a grass-fed beef operation because they had plenty of free grass and no money to spend on feed, they came to learn how much healthier their beef was and about the importance of managing the land so that they could maximize their herds of cattle, chickens, and now pigs without damaging the land. Their sustainability ethos was born of necessity, but their experiences of farming organically and the network of support and information they developed led them to more fully embrace it as their own.

Two other producers owned land and were looking for opportunities to use the land as a source of extra income. Both producers reported that they were aware of the growth of local food in the region and saw this as an opportunity to grow specialty crops such as mushrooms and microgreens. Mike and Riley Tompkins grow mushrooms on their large wooded lot, which they walked me through for the first part of our interview. Although market opportunities motivated their entry, they also spoke about how their decision to start their business was driven by concerns about the community, local economy, and sustainability:

> MT: I'm a community-oriented person. I think, you know, friends and neighbors first. Your local community, if you can help that grow, then everybody else thrives together. I mean, if you look at the bulk of our food production in this country, it's controlled by three companies: Cargill, Perdue, and . . . And it's kind of nice to know that you're employing Bob down the road, you're buying chicken from him. You're keeping him gainfully employed, and you're helping him feed his family . . .
>
> SE: In the forest you had mentioned the sustainability aspect of the business, as kind of one of the reasons why you like doing this.
>
> RT: Yeah, it's this nice complete circle, and for us I'll say it's sustainability, but it's also a multifaceted approach as we're trying to improve wildlife abundancy here, improve the health of our woods. When I talked about clearing those 550 pine trees out, a lot of them were end-of-life, because they were from back in the CVA, back when they were the Civil Conservation Corps. . . . So they [the trees] were end-of-life, and they were not doing very much besides falling down. So okay, what can we do that will improve the overall quality of the health of our forest and wildlife? So it all kind of fits nicely.

Although new farmers' entrance into local food production hinged on their moral code and often emotionally intense experiences, both were made possible by their location in the middle and upper middle class. All of the new farmers had college degrees and many were exposed to environmentalism and ethics in their education, which in some cases helped them develop an awareness of and commitment to local food. But higher education also afforded them opportunities such as internships and helped them develop social networks that they activated during their search for work or a career post-graduation, as in the cases of Melissa Harrison, Keith Stevens, and Paul Weber. In addition, many farmers' formal and informal agricultural education (e.g., attending Northeast Organic Farming Association conferences and classes or conversations with more seasoned peer farmers) exposed them to issues about the values and practices (e.g., crop rotation) about sustainable agriculture that dovetailed with the values and beliefs with which they entered local food production.

New farmers' social networks also played an important role in shaping their moral code and providing resources that allowed them to become farmers. Some new farmers' families offered financial help, access to land, or in-kind resources such as labor or marketing assistance (e.g., Melissa Harrison, Liam Cook, Ed Peters).[16] Second-career new farmers or those who became farmers in addition to their full-time job had the financial resources and even the property on which to start their local food business, and some had long careers running for-profit businesses (Rocky Top Farm, Green Pastures Specialty Crops, Mike and Riley Tompkins's Mushroomery). Yet many new farmers experienced cash flow problems, as their farms ate up most of the yearly profits, and those without non-farm jobs lived very modestly. Keith Stevens, who owns Red Maple Farm, summarized the financial challenges of growing for the local food system:

> I mean, the way I look at it economically is, if we had geared our lifestyle a little bit more to the farm rather than trying to get the farm to come up to

an income that supports our lifestyle, I might be in a little better position to be more full-time on the farm. It's a tough spot to be in. You want to have that middle-class life and a nice house and be able to take a vacation and go dancing and all the enrichments from all those things. . . . From what I see of the people who have gone full-time with farming, those are just the things that are not a part of your life necessarily, you know, and it's not necessarily to the detriment of the kids you're raising or yourself, because there's all sorts of other enrichments on the farm and the lifestyle and the community. But if you want those things, it's very difficult to pull out economically from a farm. . . . Look at Melissa and her partner [Melissa Harrison (Hidden Hills Farm) rents land to Keith and their farms are next door to one another]. They've geared how they live to the income they can get from the farm. And that's a really important perspective to take, I think, if you're going to go full-time with farming. There're very, very few people who can make a lot of money off of farming. I'm happy to say you can make a living farming here. I mean, the farm has a very solid gross income, and it's doing quite well for what it is.

In short, social class standing provided resources and opportunities that made it easier to enter the field of local food, but the costs of establishing and running their business did not always yield annual incomes to support a comfortable middle-class lifestyle.

In sum, newcomers were likely to enter farming because of a preexisting ethic about sustainability along with concerns to find a vocation that fit with their sense of self and their own aspirations for a life that would serve the good of community or society. The newcomers' moral order was a vision of agricultural work that would promote biodiversity and sustainability, minimize environmental damage to land, animals, and crops, and promote social relationships based on honesty, transparency, and trust. Stock's assessment of the moral order of midwestern organic farmers captures the vision of central New York's newcomers: "caring for the land, growing healthy food, and attempting to remake a flawed system based on instability and injustice."[17] I call the moral code on which they relied to bring this vision to fruition "critical environmentalism" because it was anchored on a set of ecological and social values that questioned the legitimacy of conventional agriculture and profit-maximization. These values also generated a set of farming rules (e.g., green composting and organic methods) and marketplace rules (cooperation, transparency about production) that would help them realize the moral order of local food.

The younger new farmers also discovered the joy and meaning of farming via their initial agricultural experiences. These experiences were emotionally powerful and provided confirmation that this activity was right and good. Unlike returning and legacy farmers, new farmers entered local food without significant knowledge of agriculture (apart from their initial internship experiences) and without the good farmer ethic the former learned from parents and grandparents. Their moral code or what we could call their agro-habitus developed through early farming experiences, college courses in environmental science, philosophy, sociology, or religion, and ongoing conversations with other farmers and customers as they built their businesses. The second-career new farmers spoke more directly about the financial motivations for entering, yet they also spoke about the importance of environmental values, and their moral code depended more on their preexisting set of ethical dispositions. In the next section, I discuss the motivations of the returning and legacy farmers, whose environmental code stresses stewardship more than sustainability.

Returning and Legacy Farmers: Stewardship, Family, and Doing What Is Essential

Seven producers returned to farming following college and/or attempts to carve out a non-farming career, while eight remained on their family farm. Among the returners, three ran CSAs and regularly sold at the region's farmers' markets; one sold her meat online and at farmers' markets; and three focused on farm sales and the restaurant trade market. Among the legacy farmers, two operated a CSA. Both of these farms operated on-site farm stands and sold their wares at a few farmers' markets. Three cheesemakers primarily sold at retail outlets; one farmer grew organic grains mainly for organic dairies in central New York (as well as selling flour and grains at farmers' markets); one sold mainly at their own farm stand; and one grew specialty produce for restaurants. Returning to or remaining on the farm was possible for those in these two groups because family land was available or they inherited it (e.g., Quiet Springs Farm, Clear Brook Farm, Valley View Farm, Black Creek Ranch). Most had a partner with an off-farm job; a few of the farmers themselves also had off-farm jobs in order to make it economically possible to farm. Those who grew up on a farm had developed the skills and knowledge of the trade as well as a set of values about stewardship of the land and/or care of animals, and like the farmers in Bruce's study

> are passionate about the social and environmental values of the food movement, and these concerns were their primary motivation for returning to agriculture. The returning farmers were also motivated by lifestyle goals, such as a place to raise a family, personal and family health goals, and because they viewed farming as a fulfilling and meaningful vocation.[18]

The farmers in my study also saw themselves as "good farmers." Many considered themselves stewards of their land and/or animals, while some embraced the environmental code of the newcomers. Most were enmeshed in strong family relationships, and working within the local food system was a means to fulfill family obligations, follow family values, and/or keep the family intact. Many of the farmers in these two categories discussed how their work helped them develop an authentic self and a self that was fundamentally moral because farming allowed them to make the world a better place. Their vision is of an agricultural world in balance that will be preserved by caring for land and animals so that both are productive for future generations, and by producing healthy food that will sustain their families and their communities. This moral vision of the good society rests on the moral code of stewardship: "the responsible use (including conservation) of natural resources in a way that takes full and balanced account of the interests of society, future generations, and other species, as well as of private needs, and accepts significant answerability to society."[19]

Many of the returning farmers spoke about how college or their non-farming careers left them yearning for something more fulfilling.[20] One meat and cheese producer with roots in a midwestern dairy family noted how her career in banking "never felt real. I created nothing of actual, tangible value. And what I was doing didn't feed my soul." Another CSA owner, Jamie Rollins of White Oak Farm, reported how her work feels like she is doing something good for society:

> I continue to do it [farming] because it's such meaningful work, it's such important work, you know. I'm not a big Rudolf Steiner person [a late nineteenth-century/early twentieth-century Austrian philosopher], but one thing that he's talked about is that one of the big problems in our culture is people can't be at their best if they don't have good nutrition. So we very much think of it that way, like, we're helping people to be better people by having better nutrition, and we get to be outside, we get to work with the land, we get to—I mean, it might be one of the only jobs I can think of that feels like entirely good for people.

Zack Jones, who grew up helping his grandfather and father on the family dairy farm, relayed a common tale of his desire to escape the drudgery of the farming life he experienced as a young person, but then realized that the grass was not greener off the farm:

> As a kid, at first you want to do everything your father did, so I wanted to be a diehard farmer. And I hit about fifteen, sixteen, and my friends on Saturdays and Sundays were at the lake or the pond, and I was milking cows, and on a tractor and things of that nature, and I wanted nothing

to do with it. So my father ended up getting out of the dairy and kept the crops. I went to college to be a teacher. About my sophomore or junior year, I realized I don't want to do this at all. I want to go back to the farm. I graduated. I got my degree and finished out, and when I came back I was doing the farm and construction on the side, and now I've switched to full-time farming.

Zack took over a small herd of beef cows his grandfather had purchased when poor health forced him to sell off the dairy herd. Zack now focuses on expanding his Angus beef herd. He spoke proudly about how he raises them without hormones or antibiotics and feeds them a diet of non-GMO (genetically modified) grain, corn, and hay he grows himself. As we sat at his kitchen table, he pointed out the picture window at the fields rising up behind the house and said how on most days he can see the cattle out grazing behind the house. He sees himself as a caretaker of the land and his animals, and believes that careful husbandry of both will produce healthy and incredibly tasty meat.

While Zack is motivated in part by the moral code of stewardship, others have more fully embraced the ideals of sustainability. For example, Nick Donovan also was deeply influenced by his family, but the animating moral code that pushed him to return to farming was environmentalism. The co-owner of Quiet Springs Farm, he grew up on an organic hobby farm his dad ran in order to provide healthy food for his family. His return to farming was inspired by his dad's model and fueled by his passion to save the environment. He and his wife, Laura (who came from a struggling dairy family), saw the emergent local food system in the region as an opportunity to follow their passions about sustainability and make a living doing so. The farm's web page notes that "good farming should support the surrounding ecosystem," and "we are farming in a way that keeps with the rhythms and rules of nature." Upon surveying the old family farm, they decided that the land was too hilly for producing vegetables because doing so would create significant soil erosion, so they opted to produce organic beef and lamb. Near the end of my interview with Laura, she responded to my question about why they keep farming despite the many challenges they face (these are discussed in the opening of chapter 1):

> Sometimes I think I'll just go be an electrician. I'll join the electrical union and go be an electrician and make a decent living and have benefits and weekends and stuff. But I don't know. I like doing something that's essential. Like, food is essential. It makes everything else you do every day possible. How much more essential can you get? But then to provide people with a healthy version of that, to take care of a piece of land, to take care of some animals, and work together to do that is really cool when it works.

The Donovans believe that farming is a social good and that it carries the weight of a moral imperative because to grow healthy and safe food means that they are making life better for members of their community. This core value, along with the goals of sustainability and stewardship (in the case of Zack Jones) and ideals about the nature of the family farm, motivates these farmers to return to this vocation. And as Laura Donovan's comments suggest, the work itself engenders feelings of joy and pride, which sustain them despite the myriad challenges of trying to make a living in a small market.

The legacy farmers are more diverse in terms of what they produce and the underlying values that guide their work. They more commonly used terms such as "stewardship" or "husbandry," and seemed more open than others to using the tools of conventional agriculture. For example, Dan Nowak, a second-generation farmer who over his career has grown sweet corn and grains, potatoes, garlic, and hops, spoke at length about his approach to farming, which emphasizes "husbandry" of soil and crops with the goal of making the land (and his business) sustainable. While he is sympathetic to organic agriculture, he wants to have every tool available in order to improve soil health, beat back pests, and grow really tasty vegetables.

But I found through doing this, even when I was running the tractor over a thousand acres, I got to really understand what it's like to keep the soil healthy. How that was going to—if you make it tasty, the profits will follow. If we do it right, everything else will follow. . . . I was husbanding this land here and it became something that I feel it now, I sense it. . . . For instance, that little [*pointing to a section of his property not far from the table where we are sitting in his backyard*]—there's some hops growing right there in that patch. It looks like just a clump of weeds there, but there's some hops that are growing there and a few other things. That's our well. And pardon me while I wax vulgar for a moment, but you don't shit where you eat. It's the old thing I heard when I was a kid. I didn't want to spray chemicals near my well. And as soon as you realize that this is an aquifer, my well is the valley [in other words, any pollution of the aquifer ends up in Dan's own well]. So, I didn't want to, and I was growing traditionally. And even when I was growing traditionally, we were using the minimum amounts of things to get the maximum effort. A lot of farmers were trained and taught to go in prophylactically and just say if a pound is good, ten pounds is better. Let's hit it and we don't have to worry about a thing, and it costs us money, but in the end we can sit back and just watch the money come in. The crops are going to be there for us. And I think that at some level that was necessary when you have one man for ten thousand acres, so to speak, you know, huge farms. But for me, I had to get out and start walking this ground to understand what was happening so that I wasn't treating a symptom that I didn't fully understand. And in the process of walking that and seeing the diseases and seeing the problems and seeing—why is this growing so well here on my right side, and on my left side forty feet away, different? Why such an abrupt change? So then I start soil sampling, and I think it was by walking out there and doing all that that this whole thing started to become synthesized into who I am.

In this extended quote, Dan describes not only how his core value of taking care of his land and crops impacts his ability to care for the health and safety of his family and customers, but also how he came to embody and claim an identity as a steward or husband of the land he had inherited. Although he notes a concern with profit, like the grass-fed farmers in Weber's study, an instrumental concern with financial well-being was not necessarily the primary motivation, but existed alongside and secondarily to other values such as stewardship and biodiversity.[21] During our interview, and the subsequent dinner I shared with his family, I learned more about his concern to preserve heritage seed stock of his garlic and hops (he makes little money from his small crop of hops, but still maintains a small hopyard to keep the seed alive), and how he regularly tests the soil and amends it in order to make sure it is producing at optimal levels. Given the great care he puts into tending his farm and his vast knowledge of soil amendments (from organic manure to minerals, to commercial fertilizers), I later asked whether he had thought about becoming a certified organic grower, and again, his response echoed the earlier themes about how the good farmer (in this case the steward or husband of the land) needs to use all of the tools available in order to realize the goal of safe and healthy food:

> The thing that I wanted to clarify, because you'd asked me if I'm doing things organically and I just want to make certain that I make my posture on this clear, that I think that organic is a tool, it's not the goal. The goal, I think, is sustainability, good health for the people that are eating the food and for the land that's providing it. . . . So, when you say are you doing things organically, I will on occasion if I think that I need a soil amendment, if I do a soil sample and I can't find a quick way to bring something in, I will use a commercial fertilizer to tweak that.

In his clarifying statement, Dan describes how his approach to stewardship will help him reach the goal of sustainable farming and healthy food but also allows him to use the tools of conventional agriculture (in moderation) if necessary. This approach was echoed by other legacy and some returnee farmers as well. For example, Scott Wilson, who was introduced in chapter 1, had produced vegetables for years with the help of chemical fertilizers and pest control, but then he discovered one year that he had depleted the soil of a twenty-acre field by only planting corn on it for nearly ten years straight. He taught himself about crop rotation, cover cropping, and zone tilling in order to revitalize that field and increase the health and efficiency of his other fields. In the extended quote below, Scott offers a more pragmatic understanding of the good farmer as he first identifies the financial costs associated with particular farming methods even as he describes in great detail the environmental benefits to land and crops of alternative agricultural practices:

> Our zone tillage,[22] the zone tiller changed the economics of farming greatly for us, both on direct cost to do it, because you can't just no-till. I tried. I tried strictly no-till. It did not work because our soil has just enough clay in it that the winters just pack it down tight. There's no planting into hard soil. It does not work. You've got to work it just enough. But at the same time, it was not economical to plow a whole entire field as had been done for a hundred years because (a) it creates plow pan, which is a hard layer that creates a soupy mess because it just holds the water, so at harvest you sink all the equipment and then you're actually doing soil structure damage; [and] (b) you plow a hundred percent of the ground, that's a hundred percent of the ground that you've got weed problems on no matter what. So you become more dependent on the herbicides. . . . And the third was the yields by using the zone tiller increased. Because in zone tilling, with the deep channels, it got the root systems down deep for a drought, so we didn't have to irrigate. In a wet season the channels drain the water off, so it kept the plants still alive, and at harvest, say a corn crop where if you had a major hurricane come through—we get those—you might see a whole entire field lay down flat and make it impossible; with the zone tillers we didn't have that issue any longer. . . . And the way we combined it with our small grain rotation, using it to [prepare for] the fall crop, we put the small grain on the field the year before. We'd harvest it, then we'd plant our fall crop, cabbage and cauliflower on that, because

the stubble, with the zone tilling into that stubble, that stubble acts as a natural weed barrier. Because we're strip tilling it, we still have solid tire tracks, so we're not doing any more soil compaction than just driving over those same spots. Our zones are good and soft still, so the cabbage is doing phenomenal.

Scott's account highlights how he moved from conventional to alternative agricultural practices, and the success he achieved with the switch reinforced the "rightness" of those decisions. Pride in his ability to replenish his soil and improve his farm led him to embrace the value of sustainability. Moreover, the experience of seeing new agricultural practices succeed over the course of a season or two may have triggered "emotional insights" in which the pride and satisfaction he felt served as cues to not only continue these practices but to reimagine what it means to be a good farmer.[23]

Other legacy and returning farmers commonly spoke about family and health concerns that drove their decisions to adopt organic methods or produce for the local market. As in the hybrid environmental-financial code articulated by Scott Wilson, a sense of duty to family and/or health concerns also motivated participation in the local food market because meeting both types of obligations was understood to be the means by which the farmer could realize profit or maintain the family farm. Both Zack Jones of Black Creek Ranch and Robert Nielsen, owner of Clear Brook Farm, returned to take over their family farms not only because their non-farm careers were bereft of meaning and purpose, but also because the older generations faced the prospect of selling the land if they did not get their sons back. And a strong sense of filial duty pushed them to return. Three dairy farmers turned to cheesemaking in part as a response to the collapse of the milk market, but they did so also as a way of keeping their land in the family and their families together. Jacob Bruckner, patriarch of Bruckner Dairy, set up a cheese and yogurt plant at his dairy in order to use the milk he could not sell because the market had bottomed out during the Great Recession. Making great cheese and yogurt (from an old family recipe) became the means to keep members of his large extended family employed, and to honor the memory of his mom and grandmother, who regularly made yogurt for the family table. The owners of Woodside Creamery ceded control of the dairy business to their sons in order to allow them to follow their dreams of farming and started a creamery making several varieties of cheeses with the dairy's milk. In short, legacy farmers constructed and identified with the "good farmer" as a steward of the land who used a variety of agricultural tools to produce high-quality produce, meats, and cheese. They also claimed to be deeply rooted to the land and worked to protect the land for their families.

Although the three groups of farmers rely on modestly different orientating moral codes, they all report the same kind of enchantment with the vocation, which helps pull them back or keep them involved in farming. Some spoke about the pure joy of the act of farming, while others spoke about their pride in what they produce and the intense satisfaction of having customers recognize the quality of their products. For example, Zack Jones noted that since returning to the family farm he has rediscovered the joy and satisfaction of farming, and suggested that the job holds the kind of enchantment the new farmers spoke about:

> I go to work and 95 percent of the time I love my job. On days when it's zero out or below and I've got to track through snow to my calves and I'm saying, "Why didn't I stick with my other job? I could be a teacher right now, warm, and not have to deal with it." But I can go out there, in the summertime especially, when you work and you sweat all day, but you look back in the day and you can see what you did. You can see it right there. We put these fences in. You're up and down the hill all over. But at the end of the day you look back and you can see your fence line and then you see the beefers going to them. You can be plowing the ground and you're there from morning till night. Then at the end of the day you look back and you accomplished something. And being able to see that and actually touch it and hold it, yeah, you did something and there's the corn

right there in your hands, there's the hay, there's the beefer that you raised from the whole time on and it's something you vision, you can grasp right there. And as a family it's what we've done.

Like most of the farmers in the study, Zack speaks about the pride, joy, and satisfaction he feels in the various tasks of farming, and these emotions reinforce his decision to return to the farm and to farm in ways that improve upon the model he inherited from his family.

Robert Nielsen of Clear Brook Farm, a returning CSA farmer-turned-baker, recalled the kinds of interactions he often had at farmers' markets with customers and how that fueled his passion for farming:

> I remember this one lady, and she had a couple of small children with her and she was trying to grab some stuff there and she didn't have a lot of money. And I sent her home with a bunch of beets. She said, "We won't eat these beets." And I said, "I'll guarantee you'll eat them. And if you'll eat them here's what else I can tell you . . . I've got three thousand times more nutrients in my beets than in your USDA beets. You'll see the difference." The next week I'm setting up the tent and she comes running up the parking lot, kids, one under the arm and one in hand. And she said, "Oh my God, I can't believe how delicious that beet was." And she said all they kept asking for was, "Mommy, can we have more beets?" She goes, "It's amazing."

He told a similar story about shopping his produce to area chefs in an effort to create an institutional market for his produce. He began this story by recounting his goals, or what he called "the prime directive" as a farmer: "grow local foods, make a healthy environment for people, don't give anybody anything we wouldn't consume," and in the spirit of Gandhi, "be the change in the world you wish to see." As he struggled with the quality of his vegetables, he began to study the soil and became "an amateur agronomist," and realized "that our whole process and how we take care of the soil even in the organic business is wrong, okay?

It's not complete. So we started doing a complete treatment of the soil, how to really diagnose the soil." As a result, the quality of his produce improved dramatically and then the phone started ringing from the chefs calling to order his vegetables:

> We would have people call back and say I have never tasted an item like I tasted from you. I've had chefs say, "I can pick your stuff out in a pile, I can see the way it cooks differently." [One chef told me] "I had my sous-chef call me back; he had two pans of stuff working and he goes, 'Can you tell the difference between these two?' And the head chef said, "I looked over and said, 'That's Clear Brook.' He said, 'You're right.'" And other chefs ask, "So what do you do?" I said, "Well, I just listen to soil." There're some pretty simple rules of life. If it's in the soil it's going to be in the plant. If it's bad, it's going to be in the plant. If it's good, it's going to be in the plant. Okay? I didn't make the rules, you just have to dance with the rules. You have to recognize what it is, diagnose what things say. And then you have to make adjustments accordingly. And so, it isn't hard to say I can see when I do a complete assay of the soil that it's lacking in these nutrients. And a lot of times, like anything else, too much of one thing actually blocks the use of something else, you see. . . . So it's easy to have these soils laden with different things that actually inhibits the absorption of other things that are important, especially the micro-nutrients, and the micro-nutrients are huge in regard to the enzymatic activities of the body as well as in that plant, and so when someone says, "Wow, it's like I'm having an experience when I eat it." It's, like, because everything is in a harmonic balance now.

These two accounts highlight how interaction between a farmer and his customers creates an emotional feedback loop that affirms his careful attention to growing healthy and tasty vegetables and thus legitimates his identity as the good farmer. Turner and Stets note, "The more an identity is verified by the responses of others, the more likely a person is to experience positive emotions such as pride, happiness, and satisfaction."[24]

The relationship between emotions and identity is somewhat complex. Happiness is a "reflex emotion" easily triggered during interaction, but once triggered, it may then cue more durable or long-lasting affective and/or moral emotions such as love and pride, respectively. These additional emotions serve as interpretive cues farmers use to evaluate self and their actions in the field and help them keep self and actions in alignment. Furthermore, this emotional-cognitive process may encourage them to engage in the type of productive work that is rewarded in the market and in emotion-laden market interactions.[25] That is, the joy and pride they experience when they produce a healthy crop or when a customer at a farmers' market praises the quality of their vegetables reinforce the decision to farm and to farm for the local market.

Thus far in the chapter I have tried to show how particular combinations of moral codes for three different types of local farmers both motivate entry into and sustain participation in local agriculture. All three groups share concerns with protecting the environment, but new farmers tend to be more strongly motivated by the sustainability and reformist moral code, while returning and legacy farmers tend to be motivated by a code centered around stewardship, family, and health. Farmers bring their moral codes with them when they enter the field, often based on education, family background, and early farming experiences, but these codes are further developed and altered as they adjust their ideals to the realities and challenges of farming, and their motivating codes often are affirmed or strengthened by the kinds of positive emotional experiences—captured in the common experience of "enchantment"—they have with the activity of farming and the interactions they have in the marketplace. In short, farming experience and farm-related interactions with customers engender emotions that help construct and legitimate the identity and practices of the good farmer, and these in turn continue to motivate ongoing engagement in the local food system. In the final section of the chapter, I examine the moral codes that organize and motivate farm-to-table chefs and restauranteurs. Although they operate with a different moral calculus, this subworld of the local food scene follows a similar dynamic regarding entry and continued participation.

The Moral Code of the Kitchen: Aesthetics, Relationships, Community

Watch enough episodes of Gordon Ramsay's *Hell's Kitchen* or read enough chef memoirs and one may conclude that morality and restaurants are at odds with one another. Yet research about chefs and professional kitchens suggests that chefs operate with a clear moral code about the nature of the good chef. In his study of several Minneapolis-St. Paul restaurants, Fine argues that they are moral communities united around shared commitments to producing high-quality food while managing the pressures and dangers that attend cooking. Moreover, professional kitchens require a high degree of cooperation, which depends on the degree to which the chefs share the same set of values about food aesthetics, culinary skills, work ethic, and solidarity.[26] Other scholars who have studied fine dining restaurants have found that chefs' moral code is anchored on a set of values and practices: quality (of ingredients and prepared dishes), creativity, innovation, and culinary skills. Lane notes that a devotion to the craft of cooking is oriented around the ability to produce "high and consistent quality of the food they serve, together with a pleasing and even exciting taste and appearance," while Leschziner contends that high-end chefs are dedicated to creating flavorful and simple dishes with the best ingredients available, and doing so "signals the chef's purity."[27] In short, the moral code of the good chef revolves around aesthetics and building a kitchen community that promotes the values of hard work, endurance, skill, and solidarity.

The handful of studies about the emerging locavore or farm-to-table restaurants and their chefs also highlights the importance of taste or quality ingredients. Two recent histories about the emergence of local, seasonal cuisine that developed in California show how concerns with taste and quality ingredients were the primary drivers of this revolution in American fine dining. Alice Waters, chef-owner of the pioneering farm-to-table restaurant Chez Panisse in Berkeley, reflecting back on her career, noted that "I was never looking for sustainable farmers or organic food. I was really looking for taste."[28] Other chefs and restauranteurs were motivated by a desire to promote more sustainable and often organic agriculture that flowed from the countercultural, back-to-the-land movement of 1970s northern California. Together a diverse set of chefs, entrepreneurs, and activists built a set of farmer-chef relationships and eventually the infrastructure that institutionalized the farm-to-table movement in California.

This movement spread east, and today local and regional sourcing for restaurants is increasingly common. As in California, taste or quality continues to be the most important value, but concerns about healthy and safe food, sustainable agriculture, and securing the economic viability of local agriculture are secondary and important values that motivate entry into and persistence in the locavore restaurant industry. In one study of over eighty locavore chefs, Inwood and colleagues found that a commitment to producing the best-tasting food possible drove chefs' and restauranteurs' decisions to purchase local produce and meats. While many chefs voiced concerns about production practices of farmers and ranchers, especially regarding the use of chemical fertilizers and pesticides, these environmental concerns were less important motivations for entry into the locavore movement than taste.[29] However, another study suggests that the kinds of environmental values that motivate the good farmers also motivate locavore chefs, especially in terms of an approach to cooking that utilizes the whole animal (commonly referred to as "nose-to-tail cooking") and a commitment to creating a food system that is sustainable.[30] Nelson, Beckie, and Krogman also discovered that the locavore chefs, in addition to valuing the quality of local produce, also reported that supporting the local farm economy and community were important motivations for embracing the farm-to-table concept. Thus, the small body of literature on locavore chefs and/or the moral code of chefs suggests that aesthetic values regarding quality ingredients and the taste of the food they create, building relationships between chef and farmer, and sustainability serve as the core features of the good chef.

Entry into local food among the six chefs and one restaurant owner I interviewed was as much accidental as driven by high-minded ideals held by many of the farmers in the study. One classically trained chef adopted local food as he learned how food choices were affecting the health of a family member. Another farmer-turned-chef opened his café because a cousin suggested they do so to sell the beef he was raising, while a third said he was driven in part by a desire to create foods he grew up eating from the produce of their large family garden. Some chefs developed an interest in and appreciation of local, seasonal cuisine while in culinary school or in early stages or first jobs at farm-to-table restaurants. Others developed a locavore sensibility as they developed relationships with farmers and foragers who would drop by their restaurant to showcase their products, and the taste and quality hooked the chefs. The moral code of the chefs in my study rests on three pillars: aesthetics, sustainability or stewardship, and building relationships of mutuality and trust between chef and farmer. As suggested above, the nascent literature about locavore chefs also emphasizes the central role taste and food quality, farmer-chef relationships, and whole animal cooking play in anchoring a new locavore culinary moral code.[31] Below I focus on the chefs at three restaurants who emphasize one of these pillars over the other two, but who are guided by elements of the full moral code.

Four chefs reported that their culinary education exposed them to the importance of locally sourcing high-quality meat and produce. Sam Cook, executive chef and owner of the Leatherstocking Inn, learned to value local foods while working front and back of the house at a variety of restaurants in the Finger Lakes wine region and the Hudson Valley. His experiences in the Finger Lakes helped him develop knowledge and appreciation of New York State wines, and his time in the Hudson Valley was especially important for developing his understanding and appreciation of locally sourced ingredients because it is one of the pioneering regions for the farm-to-table movement in New York State:

> Having been in the Hudson Valley, one of the things that I've learned there is that you have to take whatever product you have and make it a value-added thing. So if it's a dairy, they're gonna make cheese or they're gonna make milk. I mean there's places all over the Hudson Valley where, back in the late '80s you could buy bottled milk in little glass logoed things or you go to Greg Farms and pick your own asparagus.

When an opportunity arose to purchase a storm-damaged inn near his childhood home, he and his wife jumped. Once repairs were made, he turned to farmers in the area on whose produce he has constructed the new menu. He built relationships with several foragers for mushrooms and fiddlehead ferns, and several Amish farmers for produce, started a small kitchen garden on the inn's grounds for herbs, tomatoes, and peppers, and now buys mozzarella from a nearby farm that makes it from their small herd of water buffalo. Sam embraced local foods primarily because they provide him with superior ingredients for his fine dining restaurant. He spoke in glowing terms of another farm-to-table restaurant in the region but drew a clear distinction between his values and theirs: "They say, 'This was grown in the finest soil of the back-quarter acre of this property and massaged, and is exposed to two and a half hours of sunlight in the morning and seven hours in the afternoon.' I don't care about that. I want it to taste good." For him, aesthetics outweighs the locavore ethic that he satirized in the comment above. Yet, on his journey from country club day cook to executive locavore chef, he came to recognize the importance of developing strong partnerships with the foragers and small farmers who provide him with the necessary ingredients for his menu because it also is a way to build a viable local food system in a region that is known as "Death Valley" by the major restaurant supply companies.[32]

Thad Russell, co-owner of City Diner, also was exposed to local foods during his education at the Culinary Institute in the Hudson Valley, during his six-month internship at Dan Barber's Blue Hill Farm and Stone Barns restaurant, and on his first job at one of the early farm-to-table restaurants in central New York. These early educational experiences socialized him into the ideals of and provided him with the culinary skills for locavore cooking. He noted how both his formal and informal education "opened my eyes to the farm-to-table movement, and we were taught a lot about the chefs that really started the movement a decade—two decades ago—Alice Waters, Thomas Keller, Dan Barber. And they're just people, the people, the chefs that I looked up to." He and his City Diner partner, James Ellis, met while working at the farm-to-table restaurant Union Park Café when they both moved back to central New York. There they discovered that great produce is available in the region, and after a few years decided to start a more financially viable locavore eatery. They spoke passionately about how taste, support for the local economy, and sustainability led them to start up the new place and what keeps them cooking despite the financial hardships that attend new start-ups:

> TR: We weren't super impressed with the modern food chain. We wanted to kind of do our part and support local farmers. I don't want to speak for James, but at least for me, a little bit of it is a selfishness; it just tastes better. It's just a higher-quality ingredient, a better ingredient, and it's easier to work with. We were both trained in the classic French technique where you can take an okay strawberry and puree it, mix it with sugar, cook it, fold in fresh strawberries, and before you know it you have a very good product. But if you get a really good strawberry, you can just sprinkle it with a little bit of sugar and just serve it. You know, the classic, I think, Alice Waters's example of the Masumoto Peach, she just refused to do anything to it, because it was perfect. So it actually makes our jobs a lot easier to use higher-end, fresher ingredients, and that just happens to coincide with the local.

JE: There's always that subconscious feeling, too, that you feel more responsible for, and you urge the farmers—or not just agriculture, I mean meat farmers as well—you urge them to use responsible practices as well. So you've got that subconscious feeling, not only does it taste better but you feel better eating it and preparing it.... So yes, we're very into the sustainable practice not just of agriculture but of cooking.

The City Diner chefs were the most articulate about their core environmental values insofar as they talked about their concerns with food miles and carbon emissions, factory farming, and organic produce, but throughout their interview and during interviews with other chefs, ecological values tended to be expressed in terms of the culinary skills that will use all the parts of an animal or will allow them to preserve and store produce after the short growing season of central New York. Thus, they talked about their commitment to "nose-to-tail" cooking and traditional culinary skills such as pickling, rendering fat, and making charcuterie in order to make the most of whole animals and fresh local produce. Moreover, they see that creating great-tasting food is also a form of stewardship. For example, James recalled when they added headcheese to the menu:

We pride ourselves on nose-to-tail cooking. As much as we can within our abilities and skill set, we are able to break down some of these into sub-primals. . . . For example, the other day we got a bunch of really beautiful pig heads, fully intact pig heads, from Foothills Farm, and then broke it all down and he simmered it and made a really beautiful headcheese. And it's something that people normally wouldn't jump for when you come in to a restaurant, but once you see it and you realize, well, what we are really trying to accomplish here, it's pretty profound. And the flavors—once you are able to taste that mentally and physically, you realize what it is we're actually trying to do here.

They also noted how they set up their restaurant as a gastropub rather than a fine dining restaurant in order to be good stewards of the foods they sourced, because then they could have burgers as well as rib-eyes on the menu:

> I think the gastropub concept that we came up with was a way for us to kind of sleep better at night knowing that we were gonna have the ability to have a burger on the menu, because we're taking those from the same farms, so, you know, there's only two tenderloins per cow. Which is probably only three or four days' worth of steak for us, so by taking the burger from them as well, we're able to take a lot of those cuts that they grind and kind of allow them to continue to process animals and not just fall into that commodity beef trap where you just order cases of filets every week, and never—I mean, how many cows have you gone through in a year and you haven't used any of those other parts, what happens to them? Like are they being wasted?

Other chefs also spoke about their regular practices of breaking down whole animals, cellaring root vegetables, and freezing corn and tomatoes for use during the winter months. Scott Ingalls, executive chef and owner of Union Park Café, is known for turning secondary cuts of meat into mouthwatering entrees, and all of the chefs talked at length, and with pride, about the moral imperative they feel to use all of the animals and not just the choice filets. Doing so makes them into good stewards and helps the farmer or rancher maintain a sustainable business.[33]

In addition to these aesthetic and ecological values, locavore chefs also identified building relationships and community as the third pillar of the good chef code. The chefs I interviewed often spoke about their commitment to supporting local producers, although they tended to operate with a regional definition of "local." While the chefs favored organically grown produce, grass-fed beef, and the like, they also recognized that their commitment to the economic well-being of local farmers and the local economy outweighed only using certified organic produce or antibiotic-free meat and poultry as long as the products were of high quality. Thus, given the option to purchase organic produce from a different state or non-organic produce but of similar quality from in-state, they usually chose the latter. Thad Russell claimed that "we want the farmers to have quality of life," and that they are committed to sourcing locally as much as possible: "If our options are buying from a local farmer whose cattle got a little sick and he gave them antibiotics or who was having a really bad time with the drought and had to use a little bit of herbicide or pesticide on some of these products or buying organic from California or Indiana, I'd rather buy from the guy down the road, all things being equal."

The principle of prioritizing relationships over food purity is echoed by Scott Ingalls, executive chef and owner of Union Park. The list of farmers on his menu has not changed significantly in the eight years the restaurant has been open, not only because they provide him with great meat and produce but also because they are his friends. He summarized the value of relationality and his way of operating:

> You're developing a relationship, a friendship. I should be visiting the farms, and I do. They should be delivering it to me. When there's an issue, there isn't a middleman. You talk to the farmer. You got a problem, you talk to the farmer. They got a problem, they talk to me. I missed an invoice, they call me. There's no salesman, you know. I think that this isn't up to the quality that it should be, I call them and we talk. And that's really what it's all about. A lot of people say, oh you guys are that organic restaurant? Well, yes and no. I mean, most of my farmers aren't certified, and in fact, I would steer them away from becoming certified organic because it's cost-prohibitive. But they practice organics. And when people say that [we are an organic restaurant], I say, "No, I'm a relationships restaurant." I know these people. . . . I can tell you about each farm, I can tell you about each farmer. And that's what matters. And I've got their

number on speed dial. We talk. We email. We hang out. They become my friends. You know, these people were at my wedding. . . . They become your friends. And if they don't, then you're not really committed to it. And if you're not really committed to it, that's okay. Because from a restaurant standpoint, it's not really a sustainable business model in central New York.

The premium Ingalls places on chef-farmer relationships is striking given the financial challenges locavore chefs face because the meats and produce they use simply cost more, and raising prices on their menus isn't a viable option in the hardscrabble economy of central New York. Scott's former sous chefs from City Diner also spoke about placing profit below other priorities when I asked them what makes their work satisfying:

We're certainly not in it for the money. . . . It's gonna take years and years to get to the point where we're making a profit. We do it because we didn't want to work for anybody else. We wanted to express our philosophy. What's gratifying for us is that we're able to put our—literally our—product on the table, on our table and say, "Welcome to our home." And that's kind of what makes us feel like it's all worth it. When we look through that window [a window that separates kitchen from dining room] and see forty to fifty guests and you go out here [into the dining room] and you listen. . . . And if it's a tasting menu and it's super quiet, that's a good thing because they're all right in their plate. And then when we're more gastropub-y on a Saturday night and the music's up and there's a little roar in here, that's just as good.

In this statement, the chefs of City Diner articulate an ethic of care that seems to underlie the locavore chef moral code. They, like the other chefs, note that they are in the hospitality business, and at the end of the day their goal is to take care of their customers by providing them with the best-tasting food and a memorable dining experience. Chef

Cook at the Leatherstocking Inn reported that his goal is to create "a plate where you can take a bite here and like, 'Wow, that's a neat flavor,' and then you take a different bite, 'Oh, that's a neat flavor, and that's a neat flavor.' So you're creating a dish and each little piece is gonna really pop, and they're gonna go, 'Wow, that's amazing!'" Similarly, Scott Ingalls's reply to the same question I posed to the City Diner's chefs about what makes their job satisfying echoed their sentiments about a full house but qualified it by noting, "and then you add the fact that we're buying the greatest possible products that we can get our hands on and that I've made friends with the people who grow it. And there isn't any gray area. Everything is transparent here. And it's just so damn rewarding." He continued by talking about "local washing" (i.e., restaurants that market themselves as farm-to-table but have few local products on the menu and have few ongoing and mutually beneficial relationships with small growers) and his refusal to go that route (even as his business partner questioned the economics of keeping a farm-to-table place running). "Just be honest about it; it's just so much easier to be transparent about it [i.e., where his food comes from]. And when you're proud of it and when you really live it and breathe it—I just won't do it any other way."

In short, building relationships with farmers to create a menu anchored on local produce, meats, and wines is a key means of realizing care work. At the same time, as their comments suggest, a commitment to locavore cookery is tied to their sense of self and self-worth. Failing to source and cook locally would mean violating their values of honesty, transparency, sustainability, and/or stewardship and thus leave them feeling inauthentic. The pride and joy they express at running their restaurants and the degree to which they are able to follow their moral code provide an important set of emotional cues that affirm their identities and the value of the work they do as chefs. Relationships, sustainable farming, and the careful use of high-quality ingredients (all of them captured by the phrase "nose-to-tail") characterize the moral code of the good locavore chef. Ultimately, the good chef harnesses these values to prepare aesthetically pleasing dishes and create a dining experience in which their customers feel cared for. Like many of the farmers in the study, the chefs indicated that experiences of cooking and developing close ties to their suppliers cue strong, positive emotions that reinforce their moral commitment to local food.

Conclusion

In this chapter I have tried to show how the particular constellations of values held by different types of local food producers motivate and sustain involvement in this agricultural world. These constellations of values and rules, which I call moral codes, arise initially from the contexts or environments in which individuals find themselves—family and friend networks, educational and religious settings, and workplaces. My interviewees report how their more general moral or ethical orientation was developed in these contexts as families and schools, for example, oriented them toward sustainability and environmentalism or community and stewardship. Their explanations for why they entered local food production, the choices they make about how to grow or cook, and the agricultural or culinary experiences that keep them in the game are deeply moral and reflect the kinds of accounts and justifications found in popular discourse about local food. While they may not have told pioneer stories or framed their accounts as commodity biographies, their stories mirror those written by food journalists and draw on similar claims about sustainability and care for the land, taste and freshness, and the importance of relationships and community as ends rather than as means to profit.

Producers' ethical dispositions, or what others might call the moral dimension of their habitus, directed them toward getting involved in local food production. However, their moral habitus continually developed as local food producers encountered new situations and people and reflected on their experiences.[34] This is evident in the ways that farmers described sensitizing experiences such as internships on CSAs, the emotional frisson they feel while planting and harvesting, and the ongoing conversations they have with other farmers about the challenges they collectively face. As a result, their commitment to a particular kind of agriculture and agricultural ethics deepens.

The accounts of these farmers and chefs highlight the various ways values or moral codes matter, sometimes exerting a more powerful direct effect, as in the case of Liam Cook at the start of the chapter. In some cases, an initial set of enchanting experiences with farming pulls them into it as a vocation. In other cases, family, education, even religion help them develop and come to own the values that define what it means to be a good person, to do good work, to promote a good society. Values alone do not necessarily push or pull people into local food. Rather, preexisting values may prime individuals to be more open to working within a local food system or realize that the values of the local food movement in general articulate closely with their personal values. The higher the degree of fit between local food and individuals' identities as moral beings and the core values that animate them, the more likely they will be to enter the field. Once they get to work producing local food, those experiences may heighten the salience or increase the power of the values that support local food. In addition, the act of farming or cooking as well as emotionally tinged interactions (for example, the kinds of interactions chefs described regarding their relationships with their farmers or the excitement of cooking for a full and loud restaurant on a Saturday evening) may trigger positive reflex (e.g., joy, excitement) and moral emotions that reinforce the "rightness" of the decision individuals made to enter or to continue work in this field.

The case of Melissa Harrison illustrates the argument most clearly. Values inculcated by her formal education and religious upbringing orient her to be critical toward conventional agriculture, and the deadening nature of her office job makes her open to alternatives. Members of her social networks alert her to farming opportunities and encourage her to try them, and once she does, she is enchanted by the work. Farming is a joyful, meaningful, life-giving activity for her, and these emotions affirm the rightness of her decision, confirm her understanding of her identity as a moral person, and show her how her values and the values of local food neatly mesh. In the next chapter, I turn to the challenges producers face and how their moral codes help them navigate and overcome these challenges.

3

Building the Local Foodshed

Deep, raucous barking greeted me as I tiptoed my way across the rutted and icy driveway toward the farmhouse of Foothills Farm. The farm, up in the Adirondacks, overlooks a valley that seems ideal for Lori Stephenson to raise her lambs, cattle, and pigs. I was grateful to enter her warm kitchen, whose counters were filled with jars of lard (from her pigs) and a lamb in a pen. I quickly learned that the mother had rejected the newborn; Lori, determined not to lose her investment, explained that she was tending to the little one until she could return it to the pasture when the weather warmed. Lori grew up on a sheep farm but had a non-farming career before she and her husband (a native New Yorker) bought some land to homestead in the early 2000s. She began with chickens but quickly realized that she had far too many eggs for her family and began selling at a nearby farmers' market. The farm grew slowly to include pigs, ducks, geese, and sheep as her customer base expanded, fueled by the growth of farmers' markets in central New York.

Over tea and a plate of delicious cookies, I soon discovered that farming is a risky and uncertain business, and that it's not easy to move from homesteading and selling extra eggs to bolster the family income to creating a profitable business. Lori's farming skills and knowledge were dated and rusty, and she found herself on the bottom of several learning curves—where to find resources (animals, feed) and meat processors; how to breed animals and keep them healthy; how and where to sell her meat; and how to foster a loyal set of customers. The life she described is one of constant, worrisome questions: Can I recoup the up-front costs? Will this litter live or die? Can I sell all of the meat stored in my freezers before the next batch of pigs is slaughtered?

It's a lot of up-front costs. I mean, you're constantly, like, you're feeding the next batch and you're hoping to get it all sold. . . . And you're like, "Okay, I did okay here," but then you've got the next batch that's got to go and you don't get paid until the end, but you've got to pay the grain guy; you've got to pay the hay guy. And then the next batch is ready to send to the processor and I can't afford to keep feeding them because if I do they get past the right size. I had some girls this summer that by the time I got in those chops they were like fricking dinner plate size, and who can eat that? . . . And you just don't know what you're getting [i.e., the amount, quality, and portions of the butchered meat] until the end. And heaven forbid something does get sick or gets hurt and dies, you know. You're at a loss.

The costs were not only monetary. She quickly discovered that the market itself may be fickle and difficult to navigate for a small farmer. Individuals often are reluctant to pay the high cost associated with a quarter or half pig, lamb, or cow; instead they prefer to purchase select cuts. While this works for farmers' market sales, she often ends up with the extra parts no one seems to want (e.g., shanks). She has tried to sell to restaurants but has struggled to secure repeat customers. One month a chef may want her ducks or chops, but then their menus change and the orders dry up. She wondered about just how committed the region's farm-to-table restaurants are to sourcing locally: "I would like them to buy the whole animal, and I just deliver. You do what you want instead of just wanting chops. . . . If you're really a nose-to-tail restaurant then you ought to buy, like, a side of beef and use it up." She often finds herself in the role of educator as she tries to explain to her potential customers how buying a whole or half animal is more economical than by the cut or how off-cuts can be as delicious as prime cuts: "You know, you can make osso bucco with pork shank, and getting people to understand that it can be more flavorful than veal is hard."

By the end of our interview I could sense her fatigue, given the constant uncertainties and the many hats she must wear (farmer and breeder, marketer and salesperson, accountant and educator). Yet her honest and somewhat dour account was enlivened by the funny stories about the literal fox in the henhouse and the smart pigs who dragged a tree branch and pushed it onto the newly installed electric fence to short-circuit it so they could root around in the next-door pasture. Despite the challenges, farming is a joy for Lori, as evinced in her stories, the way in which she bottle-fed that orphan lamb, and the pride she voiced about raising healthy-pastured animals. Like the work of other "returners," her work is grounded in the moral code of stewardship and husbandry.

Although she cannot afford to be certified organic (she stated that organic chicken feed alone is far too expensive given the tight margins on which her business rests), she follows many organic practices. Her livestock graze on her pastures and eat hay and grains from her neighbors' farms (and she knows that they share her commitment to organic farming). The poultry forage for bugs and chow down on soy-free feed. She occasionally uses antibiotics to treat sick animals, but always tells her customers if she has: "I let it be known. And I feel that in everything, you have to have integrity. Most people will understand if you explain it to them that you're not low-dosing; you're not giving a consistent dose of antibiotics." Here she echoes the moral code of other legacy and returning farmers in which the tools of conventional and organic agriculture are put to use in order to produce healthy food in a sustainable manner. Her farm and business are anchored in the values of honesty and transparency, which are core parts of the good farmer identity. It was clear from our interview how her moral code shaped her farming practices, but her comments also suggest that the code is used to help her address different challenges to establishing and sustaining the farm. Without deep financial resources to help her weather the shortfalls and to keep her animals healthy, she doesn't always follow organic farming practices. Yet doing so means that she runs the risk of alienating purist foodie consumers, who may not want to eat meat "tainted" by antibiotics when she informs them of the treatments they have received. Her account highlights the tensions local food producers face as they try to realize a vision for alternative agriculture in a food system that favors the conventional producer and consumer.

In his study of the emergence of sustainable agriculture in Iowa, Michael Bell summarizes the myriad challenges farmers face: "Farmers must contend with an endlessly perplexing tangle of interactive and changing factors: crop varieties, soil fertility, markets, regulations, human tastes and values, equipment, buildings, access to land, access to capital, family situations, labor availability, off-farm work—and of course, the weather."[1] Individually and together, these various challenges create an imperative for local food producers to minimize or at least manage uncertainty and risk. In addition, there may be a host of job-specific skills to learn or relearn (as in the case of Lori Stephenson). Aspiring cheesemakers need to learn and consistently follow the myriad health regulations that will keep their cheese safe for consumption as well as garner the knowledge to make different types of cheeses and how to age them. Farm-to-table chefs may need to learn how to break down a whole animal and develop the skills to turn less desirable cuts of meat or little-known vegetables into culinary delights. New CSA farmers most likely will need to learn about soil fertility, pest control, and irrigation, which crops grow during different parts of the growing season, and how to ensure that they have planted enough produce to fill the weekly subscriptions for the season. In short, actors in a local food system may face environmental, knowledge/skill, and market challenges that create an unstable, uncertain, and highly risky field in which to operate.

As if these interconnected issues were not enough, they also face the daunting task of developing a new market in which the lower prices and year-round quantity of produce and meats available through the conventional agricultural system make it difficult to compete. To further heighten the challenges, they also intentionally are developing a "moral market."[2] In a moral market, the goods are imbued with explicit meanings about value and worthiness (e.g., local food is healthier or better for the environment); the way in which local food is produced makes it moral (e.g., organic practices or nose-to-tail cooking); and there are rules that govern exchange and relationships (based less on competition and instrumentality and more on cooperation and mutuality). In many ways this is an effort to create an "economy of regard," in which exchange is organized to prioritize honesty and transparency, reciprocity and relationality before profit.[3] Hinrichs notes that direct agricultural markets often are organized so that "such non-economic goals and concerns as friendship, family or ethnic ties, morality or spirituality" are given greater weight than or at least equal weight with price.[4] In other words, the producers involved in the local food market endow their goods and activities with moral weight, and include non-economic factors into the prices they charge and the experiences they offer. The challenge is that they must persuade consumers (both individual and institutional) to agree to participate on these terms.

Creating or developing a market niche within a well-established agricultural or food system is not easy. The existing infrastructure works against small producers in terms of access (e.g., few grocery stores or restaurants will purchase from small growers because it is not cost-effective) and consumer tastes have been deeply shaped by the kinds of foods that are cheap and available.[5] To create a local food market niche requires that local food producers differentiate their products, the rules that guide exchange and inter-producer relationships, and the infrastructure to market and distribute local foods from those of conventional agricultural or food markets. Local foods must be defined as legitimate, desirable, and worth the additional costs for consumers; producers must come to be seen as trustworthy and their food as safe and healthy (especially since it may not carry a USDA, certified organic, or non-GMO label), and they must be able to compete with conventional food markets.[6] As latecomers to the local food field, central New Yorkers have been helped along by a national discourse about local food, as evinced in the ways that they frame their work around health, environmental sustainability, and taste that mirror the national discourses discussed in chapter 2. This has familiarized the public with the nature and benefits of CSAs and local food, and as evident in the preceding chapter, many of the region's local food producers rely on the popular discourse about sustainability, health, and taste to sell their wares. They also have been aided by the existing networks of farmers' markets in the region and the emergence of locavore restaurants, which have boosted brand recognition and points of sale.

In this chapter I focus on how local food producers meet these various challenges as they build a new market, and to what extent their efforts are shaped by and are in accord with the moral codes that motivated their entry into the field. Creating and developing a local food market in central New York requires producers to creatively answer a host of questions about production, infrastructure, sales, and relationships with consumers, distributors, retailers, and one another. The answers they form must give rise to a stable, predictable environment if the new market is to become viable. They need to determine what to grow, how to grow it, and how much to grow, which in turn requires that they first attend to the land. Second, they need to determine the rules or norms that will govern how the market will operate, which will help producers create a market that is different from and competitive with the conventional food market. Finally, crafting market norms will help local food producers determine how to relate to one another and their customers. Developing and sustaining relationships may help create a more stable market by providing customers with non-economic reasons to participate.

Tending the Land and Managing Growth

About halfway through an episode from the first season of *Chef's Table* Dan Barber, one of the pioneering locavore chefs in the United States, offered this perspective about the importance and challenge of farming:

> If you think of soil like a bank account, many of the crops that we love require a tremendous amount of soil fertility. Which is to say, they require

a big withdrawal from the bank. Every time we eat, we are withdrawing from a communal bank. The question is, how do you make a deposit in to this bank account? You need to return fertility to the soil to get another crop. You can't count on the idea that soil will continue to give you a harvest unless you are using chemicals like most conventional American agriculture.

The local farmers I interviewed are keenly aware of soil fertility and exercise a great deal of care to improve and protect it. Care for the soil or, more broadly, the land may be the most important issue the farmers must address in order to launch and maintain a local food market.[7] How they use and care for the land will determine what they can grow, how much the land can sustain, and in general the nature and size of the market for their produce or meat. As discussed in the previous chapter, new farmers tend to rely on organic agricultural methods centered around such practices as cover cropping, field rotation, and the use of organic compost or pest controls to restore or maintain soil fertility, while returners and legacy farmers tend to be more open to using chemical amendments in a limited fashion while also adopting some organic practices, and holding firm to a stewardship orientation about their land. All types of farmers must develop the knowledge and skills to maintain soil fertility, and the learning curve for new farmers is often steep. In the remainder of this section I discuss how farmers' decisions about the soil or land open up and close off particular market opportunities and how those decisions are guided by their moral code.

I was trailing a small group of college students from a few of the region's schools on a tour of Hidden Hills Farm. The owner, Melissa Harrison, was telling the group about the history of the CSA and how the business worked, when we stopped at an unplowed field covered in clover. She explained that the farm rotates between three 1.5-acre fields and relies on letting two fields lie fallow each year. She then proceeded to explain the practice of "cover cropping" and explained how it increased the fertility of the fields. As she described the system she uses, she also noted that this was hard-won knowledge, acquired largely through experimentation:

> We have three fields and we rotate between them. Each field is in a different stage of cover cropping. . . . This is next year's field. I'm going to plow it next week hopefully, and if you look around, you tell me, what's the main thing you see? Clover. So this has been in clover since last spring. We've found, and it took many years to figure out the rotation, but the cover cropping is extremely beneficial to us. It reduces the amount of work we must do. So much happens on the off years and each of our fields is an acre and a half. After vegetables come out in the fall, we spin rye on top, and rye is biannual, so it makes it through the winters and comes up in the spring. I'm not describing this chronologically. So rye is put on top of the vegetables in the fall, so it's in rye during the winter, which stops erosion. In March I spin clover on top and that's called frost seeding. When the ground thaws and freezes it opens and closes and pulls the clover seeds under the soil. The rye is mowed in June and then the clover grows so we don't plow in between. We want to reduce tillage as much as possible. And cover cropping has reduced the weeds.

Melissa credited her early CSA internships with helping her develop the knowledge and skills to keep soil healthy and the weeds and pests at bay, and of course which crops grow best in a given environment. Although those early years of skill development were important, much of her farming capital was acquired when she had to figure out how to grow produce on her own:

> The apprentices did the hand labor, the farmers did the tractor labor. We didn't do seeding. He did all the seeding and we did transplanting, harvesting, weeding. But there were many things—cover cropping, direct seeding, tilling, cultivating with the tractor—that had to be learned when I got here. So there was some figuring out the right equipment to purchase and how best to use that equipment. So there's nuances as to

when you work the soil, how you work the soil, to keep it in its prime. Managing weeds in the off-season, managing weeds in general, in a way that is labor-minimalist. And that was big—learning the varieties that grow best for us and yield best for us so you're not wasting your time on small yields.

She noted that her soil is heavy clay, which poses its own set of challenges, most notably that wet clay becomes "like a hard rock" when it dries. "But I now understand how to work with that. You can irrigate soil. You know, it wouldn't have occurred to me to irrigate empty soil in the past. I would irrigate crops. But now I understand that hydrating the soil for the soil and then rototilling will create a much softer, easier to work with soil."

A student voice piped up and asked why she didn't have a larger farm. Her terse reply quickly ended that topic of conversation: "Yes, we never have interest in growing. I purchased the property next door in order to rent it to organic farmers. You know, in a way, renting to Keith is a different type of expanding—like it's expanding local food on this hill and improving the economy in the rural area without doing work or getting paid for it. You know, we don't want to work more."

Several months later, as we sat over cups of tea in her small cabin, we spoke more about the ideal size of her farm and why she has no interest in expanding. Her answer came at different points during our hour-and-a-half conversation and it reflects a holistic understanding of sustainability that encompasses stewardship of the land, opting out of a capitalist system with its emphasis on constant growth, and achieving a work-life balance. The CSA has 150 shares, which is the size that allows them to cultivate one field and let the other two lie fallow. "I think—you walked around with me, we have the three fields, which really benefits our growing. So if we grew the farm, we'd have to go to a two, every other year system or something like that. And really, we just don't want to work more. That's our limit." When I pressed her to expand on the reasons for limiting the size of the farm, she offered a critique about the long work hours that are normative in American society and the economic motivations that often propel long hours among the middle class. Her answer revealed her deep commitment to justice along with a concern to care for herself and her community that far outweighed putting more crops in the ground:

> There is this concept of being a "work hog," which is you are working more than you need, earning more than you need, and disallowing therefore others to do that job. And so that's part of the concept as well, for us, is limiting the amount we work. . . . At the beginning I worked fifty, fifty-five, sixty hours, and that is not sustainable for me, nor is it for many farmers. We burn out. And we have so many other interests, things that we're involved in, family and community things that we're involved in. And economically it works for us.

I followed this with a question about hiring additional workers or adopting the sweat-equity models that were the norm for many CSAs when they were established in the United States. She first noted how most of their members were white-collar professionals with limited farming skills or even knowledge of how to bend safely (a key agricultural skill) and only about 10 percent of the members were even interested. She quickly learned that the sweat-equity model would not work for her. As for hiring workers or interns, she first quoted Wendell Berry to explain why they have no paid labor: "Freedom from employer and freedom from employees. It is freedom." Her comment about freedom dovetails with the original reasons why she became a farmer, as described at the start of chapter 2. At the same time, she noted that she simply had no interest or aptitude for training novices, whether paid or not.

The other CSA operators in the study also spoke about both the imperative to manage soil fertility and how doing so impacts the size of their CSA. Like his peers, Keith Stevens of Red Maple Farm does not cultivate all of the land he rents. Only four of the ten acres are ever planted in a season. The soil is so "heavy and poorly drained" that he invested about six thousand dollars to invest in drainage to make the soil more tillable. He cover-crops the other eight, on which his neighbor periodically grazes his cattle. Using only four acres (much of it planted in a variety of fruit trees) places a cap on how much food he can produce and thus constrains his ability to expand his pool of subscribers. At the same time, Keith noted how growth was not a primary goal and was happy if the farm "fully supports itself and allows me to reinvest the profit every year." Instead, he aims to produce high-quality, certified organic fruits and vegetables for his forty subscribers and to sell at two or three farmers' markets each week. Although central New Yorkers are not clamoring for certified organic produce, Keith believes that it is important because it allows him to opt out of conventional agriculture, which is so heavily dependent on chemicals. He also noted how increasing the size would increase his workload substantially and force him to work even longer hours than he normally does. In turn, this would shorten the time he can spend with his family, which he said was more important than growing more or turning a higher profit. Thus, his modest CSA and ability to sell the extras at farmers' markets seem to hit a sweet spot surrounding sustainability and creating an alternative to conventionally grown produce, achieving a modest income, and balancing the competing demands of work and family life.

Liam Cook, of Harmony Farm, shared Melissa's ideals of limited growth and using his farm to serve the needs of the least well-off in the region. He uses a sliding pay scale for his annual CSA subscription that pegs the subscription amount to a person's income. He credits this practice to one of his mentors, Melissa Harrison, who introduced him to several business models for CSAs. One in particular captured his attention because it resonated with his concerns about economic injustices surrounding food:

> Several years ago, as I bemoaned the fact, as she did, that we seem to be subsidizing rich people's vegetables. Because my clientele, my subscribers, are privileged people. White privileged people mostly. And she and I

think along the same lines. She's been more proactive than I have. Anyway, she showed me a document that a farm in Albany had come up with, Soul Fire Farm, which is a completely non-white farming situation. And based on that, when I read it, I go, "I'm doing that." It's a sliding scale.

He also sends extra produce to a nearby food pantry and tried to partner with a community college that provides food for its low-income students (it did not work because much of the year when classes are in session, he is not growing food). As he shared his account, he voiced his own dissatisfaction with the limits of charity and inability to really push for justice: "The only thing that troubles me, and there's no solution—in the current culture we live in, there's no solution—there are people in great need. And I blame the culture for being in that situation. . . . My concern with my farm is that [either] I'm subsidizing rich white people, or I'm creating welfare recipients."

Liam's concerns about justice and sustainability as well as his critiques of industrial agriculture and capitalism were invoked regularly during our interview. This moral code seems to guide his decisions about adopting organic methods and avoiding the use of fossil fuel: "My work is mostly by hand, which is my preference—who needs fossil fuels? What are fossil fuels doing to us? Why use them? It's counterproductive. It's destructive. So I'd prefer to do things by hand. I prefer to use wheelbarrows. I have a small tractor. I till. I plow once in a while." He reported that he has been slowly learning to use organic practices such as cover cropping and composting in order to realize his vision of helping to develop a sustainable and alternative market for produce. As discussed in chapter 2, he has no interest in securing a profit or growing larger than the two and a half acres that he has under cultivation. The former is antithetical to his whole approach to farming and the latter is untenable given his commitment to working by hand. In the end, his concerns with sustainability and justice rang out when he offered a final comment about his vision for the farm: "And this is what my overall vision has been, is that I have this parcel of land and what's going to be its most elegant use so that year after year the land is in better shape than the year before. And people who live here are able to thrive without being encumbered by the dominant culture."

The farmers who produce meat must be concerned not only about the fertility of their land, but also about its carrying capacity—that is, how many animals can graze on the land without harming it. Sarah Wilson, who is the co-owner with her husband of Twin Ponds Farm, provides a representative account of how the codes of stewardship and sustainability shape her approach to land management. They run roughly forty head of beef cattle and thirty pigs on their 150 acres, and have learned that this is about as many animals as their land can sustain in any year. They produce antibiotic/hormone-free grass-fed beef and pastured pork, along with organic vegetables for sale at their village's farmers' market and at their physical and virtual farm stands. When I asked why they farm in this manner, she spoke about an imperative to grow healthy and tasty food that would be a true and better alternative to that provided by the conventional agricultural system:

> We always grew up, like my husband had said, our parents always were growing food and we always appreciated that fresh nutrient bubble.... We can see how when it's done right, how good it is for the land. And then we're watching dairy farmers go out of business and either the big guys are coming in with more liquid manure and more chemicals and it seems to be more important to balance that with what we do. And some of the stuff you buy in the grocery store is just so tasteless. We grow a lot of carrots now, and you can literally taste the difference, and any of the stuff, like, if it tastes that good and it's unadulterated, you know it's got to be better for you. And it's more filling. And then we just get people that their kids will notice it before the parents. They're like, "My kids don't want to eat. They're picky." I'm like yeah, because their taste buds are telling them that the shit in the store tastes terrible.

Sarah and her husband fell into farming as they homesteaded a twenty-acre parcel and have been learning how to manage the herds and her pastures from day one. She took classes, attended conferences, and talked to every farmer she met about best practices in order to understand how to produce organically and in ways that would not destroy the land. One of the region's agricultural nonprofits offered pasture walks to help her understand how to manage the land, yet too often she found the advice more confusing than helpful:

> So we were listening to the experts about rotational grazing. And they would say, "Oh, you've got to keep your grass at, like, six to eight inches tall for optimum nutrition." But once you start doing it in practice, the grass kind of gets away from you. And it's taller than eight inches. So I'm like, "Well, what do you do when you just can't keep up with it?" Because there's a thing called spring flush and it just—everything takes off. And he's like, "Well, bring in more cows." And I said, "Well, you can't bring in more cows because your grass is going to slow down in the summer." And they said, "Well, then you have to mow it." And I'm like, "You mean just cut it and leave it?" And they're like, "Yeah, you've got to keep trimming it." And we're like, well, that doesn't make sense because then it's just laying there and they're not eating it. So they're the experts, but some of it wasn't so practical. . . . Now we had been dividing the pastures up and we would give them an area for like a week and let them eat it right to the ground, and then we'd move them to another piece. And that was kind of like the prescribed grazing plan. And what we found was the grass would regrow, but as we went, over time, we saw more bad weeds, a lot of thistle and stuff. And it was called overgrazing.

The size of the new farm meant that they could expand their operation, yet doing so created new problems with the potential for overgrazing, and they also discovered that pigs and cattle need separate grazing areas:

What we found, for us, is when we put pigs on really nice pastures where the cows graze, they destroy it. They just rototill it. It's just inbred into them that they just got to flip that sod over. They'll graze it. And then like within an hour they're flipping it over.... So we work the pigs in areas we want to renovate.... Some spots when we first moved in were overbrush, overgrown areas, but they were flat. So we would let the pigs go in there and just destroy it. We'd level it off a little bit, put a dragger or a disk on the back of a tractor or four-wheeler, level it off a little bit and just walk away from it, see what it would do. Most of them come up with really nice grasses.... So a lot of these pig areas that we started with have now become cow grazing areas. We've extended our fences out to incorporate more of them. So then we started moving pigs to different spots. And we used to do maybe, oh gosh, fifty or sixty pigs a year. Now we're down to like thirty. We'll probably stay around thirty because it's about what—the land can handle what we've got and what we can retail. And so, it's a balance of what the land can handle, what the animals' impact is going to be and not destroy the land.

Sarah needed to learn both how to improve the land to increase its productivity and how to graze her pigs and cattle on it to maintain it while producing organic meat. She credits the development of her skills to a nine-month course with the Holistic Management Institute for women new to farming. The course taught her the basics of regenerative agriculture and grazing management, and how topography, soil, and climate must factor into decisions about how to raise animals.[8] Her story, like those of the other farmers in this section, highlights how a commitment to a particular type of farming—grass-fed and pastured meats as well as organic vegetables—shaped her approach to managing the land. In turn, this moral vision for their farm limited the size and scope of the farm. Yet managing the land is only one step on the process; farmers face a host of other decisions about sales, distribution, marketing, and building stable relationships with consumers if their farms are to become viable and perhaps even profitable.

Building a Market around Alternative Norms

During the first few months of the project, I spent hours at various farmers' markets in central New York. I thought it would be a good way to observe the local food scene and get to know its participants. At every market I visited, I had similar conversations and witnessed similar patterns of farmer-shopper exchanges. First, after I introduced myself and my research, a farmer or a shopper would inevitably point out which sellers were truly local and which were selling produce trucked in from outside the region. And they often did so with scorn, anger, or disbelief in their voices. As I chatted with a berry farmer one afternoon, she suddenly raised her arm, pointed across the market to a large tent, and snarled, "That guy is selling peaches in June. There's no way those are local." At a different market a farmer shared how some vendors advertised themselves as local farmers, but if I were to take a quick look at the boxes at the back of their truck I would see that the produce was certainly not coming from local farms. At most of the markets shoppers readily identified the sellers who were reselling produce bought at wholesale and often from Pennsylvania, and those who grew their own produce nearby, and then urged me not to buy from these vendors. It was apparent that those involved with the market had a clear understanding of what local meant and that they expected farmers to be honest and transparent about their produce. My early observations at the region's farmers' markets indicated that shoppers and farmers shared a set of values and norms that guide how the local food market should work. In this section of the chapter, I describe these norms and how they help local food producers create a particular type of market distinct from other food markets.

Much of the literature about the rules and practices for farmers' markets and other forms of direct agricultural markets (i.e., those in which producer and consumer are in face-to-face contact) reports similar findings about the centrality of honesty, transparency, and authenticity.[9] Some markets have formal rules requiring that vendors grow their own food within a particular geographic area (for example, Ithaca's farmers' market, which is not included in this study, requires that vendors farm within a thirty-mile radius of the market space). More generally, scholars have characterized local food markets as part of a "moral economy," in which "the local is assumed to enable relationships of aid and trust between producer and consumer, eliding the faceless intermediaries hidden within commodity chains and industrial foods."[10] Some claim that local food markets promote community, cultivating an "ethical subjectivity" among producers and consumers in which trust, generosity, and even affection displace or at least override purely economic interests.[11] More generally, a moral market is one in which human needs and the goals of extending human freedom and flourishing, as well as preserving the integrity of the environment, are placed above profit and the operation of a supposedly free market. In one of the pathbreaking essays about alternative agriculture, Jack Kloppenburg and his colleagues highlight the difference between the conventional and the alternative food systems:

> The global food system operates according to allegedly "natural" rules of efficiency, utility maximization, competitiveness and calculated self-interest. The historical extension of market relations has deeply eroded the obligations of mutuality, reciprocity and equity which ought to characterize all elements of human interaction. Food production today is organized largely with the objective of producing a profit rather than with the purpose of feeding people. . . . The moral economy of the foodshed [i.e., alternative agriculture] will be shaped and expressed by communities. . . . We imagine foodsheds as commensal communities which encompass sustainable relationships between people (those who eat together) and between people and the land (obtaining food without damage).[12]

The local food market in central New York is organized around these ideals and the alternative set of norms or rules that govern behaviors of and relationships among participants inspired by those ideals. The norms help producers position themselves to compete with conventional food markets because they offer something more than a low price, and they also help them establish the rules of the game that will ensure some degree of stability and certainty. The rules of the game are built on three normative pillars: honesty, transparency, and cooperation. Together they help farmers minimize competition within the market and build a stable set of customers, who in turn give them their best chance to compete with conventional supermarkets.

Honesty and Transparency as Guides to Market Exchange

At the region's farmers' markets, both consumers and the truly local farmers followed norms of honesty and transparency. As discussed in the opening vignettes of this section, farmers who tried to pass off their produce as local were discredited in the eyes of other farmers and some customers because they were not considered honest or trustworthy. And for some consumers, this made their produce less worthy and assumed to be inferior in quality. For example, during a long conversation with a transplanted Long Islander, she emphasized the importance of trust between farmer and shopper:

> So I found out about [a local farmer] and he seems like a very trustworthy person and I always make sure I see the person. I even go to the back to see them, to see what's going on and talk a little bit and see if he is authentic and honest. He has authentic food and great food. That's what I know. It is trustworthy, it's a great product, you are excited to go and get it, and when you go and eat it, you are going to have a great experience.

I commonly witnessed farmers explaining how they followed organic practices although they were not certified by the USDA and did so in order to be as transparent as possible, as suggested in this comment from a cheesemaker, Ken Allen, with whom I spoke: "I've had a lot of customers ask about organic and I'll tell them, I'll go, 'You know, I'm very close to organic. If I have a sick cow I'm going to treat her." And I'm going to tell you that I'm going to hold her far beyond the recommended amount of time." One afternoon, one of my students and I were helping Keith Stevens at a farmers' market, and we watched him patiently explain to customers how organic fruits and vegetables were different from non-organic. When a regular customer stopped by and asked Keith for advice about how to keep the bugs out of her home vegetable garden, he proceeded to explain various organic pest control techniques and products that he uses. Reading my fieldnotes long after this exchange, I was struck by how it embodied the core values of the alternative market: transparency, educating the public to more deeply understand food, and building relationships. During our interview I asked him why he decided to be a certified organic grower. His reply highlights the strong norms of honesty and transparency that guide him and others in the local food market:

> By being certified organic, I think that I can sort of stand there at a farm stand and tout my stuff as organic, and not feel any guilt with my neighbor, who is perhaps selling really good local produce but it's not organic and, "Who's this guy over here saying he's organic when he's not certified?" I'll never have to deal with that. I'm certified. If you have any qualms or questions about my farming practices, come to the farm, talk to my inspector as well, and you'll see where we are.

His justification mirrors Lori Stephenson's explanation about the use of antibiotics when she sells her pork or chickens. Such acts of selflessness and potential disregard for one's own profit were common among the farmers I observed at the markets and whom I interviewed.

Creating a Stable and Predictable Market through Cooperation

Cooperation was the third norm upon which the local food market rested. Working together to create an alternative market helped build solidarity and community internally and limited local food producers from competing with one another for the relatively small pool of customers. Cooperation took on a variety of forms. At the farmers' markets, for instance, market managers reported that they limited the number of each type of producer in order to minimize competition:

> I talk to applicants about our market and let them know that I don't know if our market could support another vendor like them because we already have vendors who sell meat or who sell eggs or something else. A lot of them do understand, because they need the market to be beneficial for them, and they tell me that they don't want to have to compete: "I don't want to compete with other guys who grow beef and chicken. There are already three or four at the market." And so, in some ways, there are, I think a number of farmers would be interested. And yet, they're, looking for other direct marketing outlets, rather than the farmers' market just to avoid a problem.[13]

Many of the CSA farmers in the study jointly purchase supplies such as compost, seed potatoes, or fertilizer in order to save costs on bulk orders. Several run farm stands and not only sell their own produce but sell the meat, produce, or value-added products such as jams or pickles of other farmers. They regularly talk (often virtually) about farming issues or needs that arise during the growing season, and periodically gather for meals. Jamie Rollins of White Oak Farm noted, "I think very much it's been part of the organic farmer tradition to be very supportive of each other and try to share information and help each other out as much as we can." As discussed in the opening vignette of chapter 2, Liam Cook learned a great deal about how to run a CSA and how to farm from conversations with Melissa Harrison of Hidden Hills Farm as well as Jamie Rollins of White Oak Farm and the owners of Three Willows CSA. He noted how they "share ideas and bounce things off of each other. Sharing resources and failures is crucial." Keith Stevens reported that this loose network of CSAs "work together and share stuff and try to bring customers to each other." Melissa Harrison added that members of the network commonly trade items during the season when they run short for their weekly baskets or have too much of a particular crop: "I have five hundred pounds of potatoes, does anyone need some? Or I'm running short on my CSA. I need a hundred pounds of beets, does anyone have some?"

These examples highlight cooperative norms about resources, information, and customers among farmers and created a greater sense of certainty and stability.[14] Few of my interviewees saw other farmers, chefs, or cheesemakers as competitors to be bested; rather, they were neighbors to be helped. One of the chefs at City Diner captured this norm in his answer to my question about the future of local food in the region:

> We would never look at some of the other restaurants around here and say, I just wish I had some of their business, or I wish we were doing better than them. I would never say that because the better they do, the better we do. The better the guy down the street does, and the more responsible sourcing that they do, the more we are going to do. Because that helps the local farmer and that makes them more successful and more able to have the means to supply all of us. So it's, as the tide kind of rises there, we're able to find newer, or even some producers that have been around for thirty or forty years that we didn't even know about, because we're able to showcase them to other restaurants as well.

Cheesemakers Ken and Barbara Allen used the same metaphor of the "rising tide" to describe their relationship with other cheesemakers in the region, and like the City Diner chef believe that more participants in the market will make local food more resilient:

> There's that old saying that "a rising tide raises all boats." And I think for the most part we've all recognized—I don't feel at all threatened by Sweet Clover Creamery. I don't feel at all threatened by Bruckner's because I

really think that there's enough people to buy. And the more producers that are doing this, that are delivering a good product, the more they're going to tell their friend about a local farm and that person could be two hours away but might look in their neighborhood to find their own thing.

In short, cooperative norms and working against competition are grounded in the shared understandings of what it means to be a moral person and how to behave ethically in the marketplace. According to some scholars, cooperation is "the most pervasive value" that organizes how farmers' markets operate.[15] At the same time, cooperation reflects another key value that has shaped the formation of the local food market: relationality.

The Central Role of Relationships and Community

Adhering to norms of honesty and transparency in market transactions helps local food producers develop relationships with consumers. They also engage in a number of practices that aim to build relationships by embedding consumers or customers in community. CSAs have long been touted as the means to reconnect farmer and consumer and create a community bonded by shared risk and reward and affective ties between farmer, consumer, and place. Community is built into the business model of CSAs insofar as it requires consumers and growers to make a months-long commitment to one another. Typically, consumers pay for their weekly box of produce (and in some cases meat and/or fruit) before the growing season starts. The up-front payment model provides farmers with reliable financial resources as they plan for the upcoming season and creates a relationship in which consumer and farmer share both the risks and rewards of producing local food. Durrenberger notes that "a CSA is a way to bind people into a tight social group together through shared effort, travails, and gratifications of producing their own food."[16] Some CSAs require members to work on the farm (a form of sweat equity) and others host social events such as meals or farm walks, both of which help deepen the connections between farmer and consumer.

Most of the CSAs in the study and a few other producers saw their work as building community, developing relationships with customers, or offering opportunities for consumers to develop relationships with one another. For example, Kate Owens, co-owner of Sleepy Hollow Farm, explained how their CSA was formed around a core of families who collectively and with the owners decided what to plant. They also provided significant labor during the first few years of the farm:

> We started out with maybe five different families. So we just kind of decided as a group, you know, what, what kind of produce we wanted to have, and then also families signed up to buy portions of different animals that we are raising. So we started out just doing custom butchering, where different families bought in together on cow shares and pig shares. And so that worked out. It was a lot of fun, was super intimate, and families came out and we harvested food together, everything that was harvested equally. . . . We did that for two years. And then the third year, we switched gears to try to lighten my workload . . . to doing one year of all you-pick. The first couple years it was, you know, occasionally, people will come out a little bit, but it was really more of me trying to teach the kids, you know, how to do stuff. So I really tried to put people to work. And there, you know, there were some people that were very into it. I found that that was probably about half of my core group that I kind of built up.

Several others have tried the sweat-equity model but have discovered that only a small number of their subscribers wish to participate and have moved toward more periodic farming events such as garlic planting and harvesting. These are annual events at Harmony Farm and Hidden Hills Farm as well as at farms that specialize in garlic (e.g., Lucky Acres, Ridgeline Farm). Liam Cook at Harmony Farm described the ways in which the major planting and harvesting events help build relationships and arouse the kinds of positive emotions (pride or joy) and sense of enchantment that create bonds of people to the farm and one another:

> Big things like garlic planting and garlic harvest, which are really big jobs that happen all at once. Potato planting, potato harvesting. Onion planting, onion harvesting. Some of the best times are when we have—actually the last three years the garlic planting has been such a hoot because we get ten or twelve people and we just have such a splendid time. And we look at our work when we're done. "Isn't that pretty?" And as I say, it just deepens everybody's appreciation for what's going on. And I can't think of anything better.

When I asked Melissa Harrison about the ways that her CSA promotes community, she spoke at first about events such as the garlic harvest, apple pressing, and the recently added weekly yoga classes. As she continued, I heard a more nuanced, almost ethereal account of community. Community is less like a tight-knit group of like-minded friends and more akin to a felt belonging to the land and those who work it.[17] The farm is a place where one feels at home; it is a place of renewal for self and family; it is a place that engenders joy, which in turn deepens the sense of belonging to Hidden Hills:

> I would say 80 percent feel like they're part of a community. I would say, not that they all come to events, but there's a relationship.... I would say I know 80 percent by name, they know us, and they've been here for years and whether or not they come to special events—the people who come to special events are more minimal. It's a smaller group that comes to the work parties. But you know, when we do the cider pressing, even though it's a large event and like eighty people might come, a lot of them aren't members.... It could be old members or people who had an interest but never joined. But I still think that people feel like part of Hidden Hills Farm. And when they're here, they're interacting with other customers, and I have also noticed in the last few years the pick-your-owns I allow

anytime during the daylight. And more and more people are coming by themselves on the weekend just to pick some flowers or just to be here by themselves and just be in the space. . . . Many people say it's the best part of their week to be outside with their kids breathing fresh air and it's under the sky and not in the office. And that's important to us too, to provide this space as a community space. To be outside with purpose. There's not much that our culture has for people that's being outside with a purpose. I've always treasured this place and I want to share it and I feel really happy when other people are getting joy from it.

The partial, loose, or episodic nature of community that local food producers create mirrors the findings of other studies about CSAs. A 2010 study of New York State CSAs found that community was an ancillary motivation to join and few members reported feeling integrated into a local food community. Similarly, a more recent study found that "CSAs are not perceived as real, tangible communities by their members, although they hold the potential to become so." Some CSA members feel like they belong to an invisible or imagined community.[18] Increasingly membership in a CSA or shopping at a farmers' market is often guided by instrumentalism and convenience rather than a search for community and relationships, and this poses significant challenges for creating and sustaining community. In addition, the imperative to cultivate a sense of belonging among customers must be balanced by other needs such as ensuring that there is enough produce to fill the weekly boxes during the season and to make delivery or pickup consistent, convenient, and low-cost.

Meeting all three goals is quite difficult, as Paul Weber, who runs Stillwater Farm, discussed during our interview. He began by trying to replicate the diversified CSA model from his internship years in New England (i.e., a CSA that provides as much as possible of the food for a family's weekly intake—vegetables, fruit, eggs, dairy, and meat—while using only human and animal power). His involvement with this CSA gave him an idealized vision of community because it served a fairly small town where many people already knew each other. He smiled as he recalled the Friday evening pickups because "everybody just showed up." However, his CSA served a larger population and wider geographic area, which worked against the development of community:

> I think right away it didn't build the community that we saw happen in New England because here people didn't even know each other, so often we'd see people come in and they would talk to us. So there was that, the community of people that we were growing that were our friends but not necessarily friends with each other. But over time, you know, we would definitely see people come in, they'd meet each other here, because they would talk about, "What is that that you're grabbing?" "Oh, this is the store's kohlrabi." So people would get to know each other and they'd swap recipes, and that was really cool. And we did things to try to facilitate that, or to try to grow that. For sure, nobody really got into it. We had a recipe board, like an online thing where people could share recipes. And we did a whole central New York milk map, where people could carpool to get milk together. But it just never took off the way I wanted it to.

Paul continued by commenting on the challenges of finding the right business model that would encourage community while allowing him to do the kind of farming at the scale he wanted. He learned quite early that running a diversified CSA is a tremendous amount of work in which adding members requires putting more land in crops and adding more animals to maintain the full share, and he learned that he simply doesn't enjoy some types of agriculture. Over the next few years, he experimented with different crops and animals and different CSA models, but in the end, none were very effective at building community:

> I think, just like a lot of farmers, you know, we kept making it more and more convenient for people. So instead of having that one day to pick up, we now had five days. So, you know, instead of seeing that person every Thursday, you might see them every week but you might not. And

so many growers now, they're just doing the produce season. You know, they deliver to a drop spot, and the drop spots are there all day—a coffee shop—and you stop by. But there's nothing wrong with that in general, but as far as community is concerned, I think it's harder to foster community.

While fomenting community and encouraging relationships between farmer and consumer remain important goals for Paul and the other farmers in the study, he found that he was not able to effectively create and sustain community on his own. Paul eventually oriented his farm to produce primarily for restaurants (although he still sells his raw milk and beef and pork to individuals, and many are his original CSA subscribers) and now runs a restaurant-supported agriculture (RSA) business in which the relationships he forges are with chefs. The turn toward supplying restaurants was not easy, as it "is as topsy-turvy as the farm business." However, he has developed several farm-restaurant partnerships that have made his business more stable, predictable, and profitable. One of his most important customers is Scott Ingalls, owner and executive chef of Union Park. Their families have ties extending back two generations, and Paul says that Scott Ingalls "is actually like an old family friend." They work together to plan out the vegetables and meat Scott anticipates needing, and, as Scott explained to me during a special wine dinner planning session he invited me to attend, "We build our menu, not just the special dinners, but each week, around the vegetables that are available. And from there we decide what protein pairs best with the veg." Paul noted how fulfilling and challenging their partnership is compared to some of his other clients who place large orders for only a few crops like tomatoes:

> He's really committed to local food and he's interested in trying different stuff. And his menu changes all the time so he really can take advantage of the seasonality of our food. And he's been around long enough that he's solid enough that we feel like we can rely on him and we've been around

long enough that he can rely on us. . . . Union Park is much smaller than Gotham Diner [another restaurant he supplies], and so sometimes it's challenging to grow all these different vegetables that they're interested in, and have something new and fun every week. Because then you're managing a hundred crops instead of, for Gotham, five. But he is so willing and excited to shift around whatever we have. So that's really great. We're doing more and more with Union Park every year. They're actually buying more and more of our beef now, which is great. He really is good about using other cuts to do a lot of the—I mean a smart restaurant chef like Scott knows that, "Hey, I can take this cheap cut that nobody wants to buy, and the farms are all selling it cheaply because nobody wants them, and I can turn it into something that's delicious."

In this extended excerpt from our interview, Paul describes a relationship built on cooperation, mutuality, and trust. The farmer provides the resources by which the chef can realize their mission to produce high-quality and locally sourced food while guaranteeing that the farmer will be able to sell their organic vegetables and pastured meat. There seems to be a symbiotic relationship between farmer and chef in which they help each other adhere to the moral code that guides their work. Other chefs also spoke about how a core set of providers allows them to realize the farm-to-table ideal. For example, the chefs at the Leatherstocking Inn and at City Diner list their "primary local farm partners" on their menus, and the former also shops at a nearby food co-op that "carries a tremendous amount of local stuff." In addition, he supports two cheesemakers, a mushroom forager, and the honey produced at a dairy nearby. For Thad Russell of City Diner, the restaurant's success rests in part on developing relationships of trust with the region's farmers and supporting the local agricultural economy: "Really for us as a small restaurant and working with small farmers, it just comes down to meeting the people, asking them some questions and really trusting them." Similarly, Laura Donovan of Quiet Springs Farm noted how the local food system rests on relationships of trust that can be developed only through face-to-face relationships. And like the locavore chefs in the region, she feels that the relationships and the local identity matter far more than a particular set of agricultural practices:

> We have people at some of the farmers' markets that we've had a relationship with for a really long time and they buy from us because of that relationship, not because we have a certified organic stamp on our stuff. You know, we had people that would call from New York City and they're like, "Hey, we want to buy some of your beef, are you certified organic?" We're like, "No we're not, but we have organic practices and we're certified naturally grown." And they're like, click—they don't want to talk to us because they need that assurance [of the certified organic label]. Because they can't have a relationship with us. My customers know what I do because they've been to the farm.

Thus, the moral market local food producers seek to create is organized around a set of norms that help build relationships of trust between consumers and farmers, as well as among producers themselves. These norms and the degree to which farmers and consumers form a community, whether imagined or episodic, help make the market more certain and stable. The normative order of the market also imbues it with extra-economic meaning, as buying and selling local produce, meat, and cheeses help participants realize non-economic goals such as slowing global warming or eating in a healthier manner. At the same time, the normative structuring of the market limits the size and viability of this alternative market because many consumers cannot participate or choose not to participate.

Intractable Market Challenges and the Moral Codes of Local Food

Despite their best efforts, local food producers face a set of challenges that seem difficult if not impossible to solve. These problems arise from the size of most local food operations. The small scale of most producers, especially those who specialize in meat, makes it difficult for them to gain access to institutional buyers (such as restaurants and wholesalers) and meat processing plants. In addition, their small size and commitment to organic practices often make the costs of production higher. Laura Donovan of Quiet Spring Farms summarized the scale problem for local meat producers in the following exchange:

> LD: You've got a small number [of meat processing plants] and the availability, like, geographically, and also just the scale that we operate at is small and so it's difficult—like right now for the beef we're processing this year, and next year even, we're trying to make an appointment for that because it gets that full. And we could have all these animals in the field but to get them to the processor and get them processed in a way that we can retail them, sometimes that's out of our hands. We'll be on a waiting list. We had pigs that were ready to go last summer and we were on a waiting list to get an appointment—and waiting and waiting and waiting.
>
> SE: Is that because there's just two USDA processors?
>
> LD: There are, and then we're small. . . . We call them and they're like, "We're booked." Because they're booked on speculation somewhat, because everyone's trying to beat that problem. . . . You've got to use a USDA-inspected processor to retail. We've got a great little place just over the hill that will take you anytime, but they're not USDA-inspected so we can't retail that stuff. So yeah, that's a problem. Legally you can't. Like, for me to go to a farmers' market and say, "Here's a steak I raised and packaged, this much per pound," it has to be USDA-inspected. It's a huge constraint. I understand why it got started, but I think the only difference between this little custom place over the hill and that place up there is that there's not somebody that works for the government in a white coat who says, "Yeah, this was done the right way." . . . It adds cost, it adds time, it reduces flexibility. It adds a lot of cost. You know, we've got to haul to

Pennsylvania or to Stamford, or, like, we have Bridgewater here, New York Custom Beef, which is great, but they're a little limited with what they can handle.

The small scale of Laura's operation combined with the limited number of available processors and number of producers scrambling to get their meat processed makes it difficult for Laura to efficiently get her meat to market. Nick Constantino, a meat and value-added expert who works for an agricultural nonprofit in the region, summarized the access problems that small farmers face:

> That's where economies of scale come into place. Most of your farmer-vendors at farmers' markets, they're only slaughtering, like, a small volume of animals at a time, which they pay the full shot to get their meat processed. That's why it's such a very hard business to do. . . . We don't have a processing infrastructure that can deal with local foods because you don't have the volume or the demand. Like, if someone was going to say, "I can use 500,000 pounds of sweet corn." Okay? All right? So now I know it's sold. Now you can build the infrastructure to handle it. But to invest in equipment is ridiculously expensive. Handling costs are ridiculously expensive. Labor is too. So if you don't have the volume and a guaranteed sale, you can't even think of investing in it.

In many ways the size of most local farms significantly decreases their ability to compete in wholesale or restaurant markets because they cannot provide either the volume or the price to meet the demand. Meat processors need the guarantee of high-volume partners if their venture is to succeed, which makes them reluctant to take on or even prioritize small farmers. At the retail level, both farmers and restauranteurs face different pressures that often preclude forming an ongoing relationship. Lori Stephenson spoke about her struggle to find reliable restaurant buyers: "The hard part, when it comes to wholesaling for most of us [is] that we are small, but need to get a fair price for our meat. We're already such a tight margin and of course the restaurants, they need a lot of it. Like, if you're trying to get a chap to buy from you who has been ordering his meat from Sysco, I usually can't even come close to those prices, you know." Other farmers reported similar problems with access to restaurants as chefs often want only choice cuts or won't use less desirable cuts of meat, and most commonly their reluctance to buy off-cuts stems from the demands of their diners. Most of the chefs I interviewed commented that their best sellers are filet mignons or other choice steak cuts, yet a single cow will yield only a small number of filets. Scott Ingalls from Union Park highlighted the dilemma from the chef's side:

> People like filet mignon for what it is: tender, expensive, a sign of haute cuisine, you know? So it has to be a center cut. It has to be circular. And if you've ever seen a tenderloin [*holding his hands apart to show me the size of a tenderloin*], it kind of tapers to this end, so you have to cut from here, and then up here it gets real fat and you've got the head, so you can't cut from here. So you've got what you call the center cuts. And that center of the six-pound tender is probably about two pounds. Now I'm shooting for a seven-ounce filet. . . . One, two, three, four. Okay, so there's two tenderloins on a cow. So let's say I got eight portions from a cow. One cow gave me eight center-cut filets. I'm selling between sixty and ninety pieces a week. It's my best-selling entree. So that's a lot of dead cows. It's a lot of cows—I don't serve a burger!

Zack Jones of Black Creek Ranch, who raises Black Angus cattle, described the scalar issue he faces, and his comments echo those of Scott:

> The biggest issue in restaurants is the steaks. Because my average steer weighs eight hundred pounds, hanging weight. Out of that whole thing there's forty pounds of premium steaks, which is your strip, your filet, and then your Delmonicos. Your average steak, if you get a T-bone some-

where it's usually a pound, right around there. So if you get forty pounds of that stuff, and then you have quite a bit of the other. And most restaurants don't want the other cuts. Well, they don't want the burger. They will, but not on the demand. They'll do a top round and make a roast beef type thing and have it for a special, and that is some of the other. But the biggest issue is you've got a lot of pounds and they only want forty. My cousin went and talked to a guy he knows who owns a high-end restaurant. And they go through four loins in a weekend. That's two steers a weekend.

His herd is not large enough to supply even one restaurant with the steaks they need, and given the two-year time frame to grow a calf to its slaughter weight, the cost of calves to expand his herd, and the limits on the carrying capacity of his land, he cannot easily scale up. As a result, most local farmers rely on direct markets (i.e., farmers' markets, farm stands, mom-and-pop retail outlets, or online sales). Yet here they run into what many called the "low-hanging fruit" problem. The primary customers for local foods are the middle- to upper-class "foodies," but farmers have discovered that persuading non-foodies to buy local is more difficult. For example, one afternoon I was chatting with Lori Stephenson at her farmers' market stand when an older shopper stopped by and asked about the price of her pork chops. When the customer heard that the chops went for $9.99 per pound, she huffed and said, "I can get them for just two or three dollars per pound at Price Chopper [a northeast grocery chain]. Why should I pay so much for your chops?" Rather than try to answer this question, Lori just politely suggested that the shopper head over to the grocery store. The shopper walked away with a puzzled and somewhat angry look on her face and Lori shrugged and said that life was too short for such conversations. Another beef producer, Dave Robbins, the owner of Rocky Top Farm, wryly noted how his own mother doesn't want to pay the prices he charges: "I'm like, 'Mom, whatever you want I'll drop it off once a week. Come to the farmers' market and I'll have it ready for you.' So she came once and she insisted on paying and I wouldn't charge her. I said, 'Mom, it's the least I can do, you're my mother.' 'I'm not paying that much for chicken.' Or 'How much are pork chops? I can get that at the supermarket for $2.39 a pound.'"

Thus, a buying public generally accustomed to low food prices is a second challenge farmers must address. Laura Donovan spoke at length during our interview about the difficulty of competing with the low prices of conventionally grown food and the need to combat this via consumer education:

> The ninety-nine-cent ground beef doesn't reflect the cost of production at all. You know, there are subsidies in place for the feed and the trucking and the manufacturing, and they used probably labor that wasn't treated fairly. So there's all of that that comes out of it, that people only see the sticker in the store, and then they see my ground beef is ten dollars a pound and they just think I'm trying to get rich. I'm happy to write blog posts as much as I can, and talk to our customers, . . . but the onus for the education has really been placed on the farmers, and we don't have that much time in the day.

Many of the participants in the study remarked about the need to educate the public about the benefits of local food and the true cost of producing it, and to dispel myths about organic or local agriculture. Yet few had the time to engage in education, and among those who tried, their efforts often were limited to blog or web page posts, or one-off conversations with a customer at a farmers' market. For example, White Oak Farm owner Jamie Rollins responded to my question about the degree to which she tries to educate the public about CSAs and local food by noting the limited time she has for this task:

> Yeah. I don't know how much time I spend—I mean I just put out my stuff—you know? And then say what we're doing. I don't really have a lot of time for purely educational work. Well, I would say farmers just don't

have time. I don't have time. You know, like, I definitely do spend a lot of time writing newsletters, explaining recipes, interacting with people in the distribution room and stuff, but those are people already in my CSA. Like, I don't have time to go out and, like, spend a lot of time with people who aren't on board already.

Locavore chefs and restauranteurs face a particularly daunting challenge because anywhere from 35 percent to 50 percent of their diners are not locavores. A heavy-handed attempt to educate their diners could backfire. The chefs called many of these customers "filet mediums," by which they meant the diner who wanted their steak dinner cooked medium and were only dining out for a fancy steak dinner. Scott Ingalls of Union Park angrily commented, "In this goddamn farm-to-table [restaurant], my best seller is the filet mignon, and it is the only protein in this building that isn't locally sourced." Like the other chefs, he lamented that so much of his trade did not contribute to sustainable agriculture or help farmers more, but he was aware that overdoing locavore education during service might drive away customers:

> If you're not careful, you could come off as really highfalutin. That cheese plate that we go through and talk about all of it? People can be downright offended by that. And that's their right. They don't have to want to hear that, they don't have to care about those cheeses. They might be here for a filet mignon and a bottle of expensive red wine from Napa Valley. I can serve that. So the server has four to five minutes at the beginning while giving the features and taking the drink order to decide, what are you here for? And if you're here for a business meeting, four filets and a bottle of red wine, leave them alone. Let them be who they want to be. Their money's green, you know.

The chefs at City Diner spoke about the need to tread lightly on educating the palate of diners while holding true to their nose-to-tail/sustainability moral code:

We did the headcheese, and the five or six that we sold of those all last week, those people—most of them very much enjoyed it, and even the people that maybe will never order it again were still very appreciative and excited to experience it. But to just put something out there in an area that doesn't have maybe quite the adventurousness with food as some of these larger urban city centers, it's tough. So we try to sort of thread the needle between doing some offerings like the headcheese and seeing how people go, and then potentially using some of those off-cuts and foraged things on menu items that have more attractive items. So, for example, our Backpackers Lunch, if we were to replace the pork sausage with the headcheese, maybe nine out of ten people wouldn't even try the headcheese.

The chef at the Leatherstocking Inn takes an even more understated approach. He lists his farm partners on the back of the menu because he wants to "normalize the idea that we work with farms, but we're not gonna tell you everything about the farms or their products." He echoed Scott Ingalls's concern about how to balance the competing demands posed by an ethos of hospitality and an ethos of locavorism:

It's [educating diners] one of those things where you do it in little bits and pieces. And the people who are interested will ask. The people who are just here for—you know, "It's our fiftieth anniversary so we're going out to dinner, and I'd like my steak well done please." Those people, I don't wanna sit down and try to tell them how amazing this local product is from this one guy who grows these mushrooms in his closet or something like that. That's not our style.[19]

The challenge of competing with the low food prices in conventional supermarkets is exacerbated by the structure of the US food system itself. The majority of food sales in the United States take place at supermarkets, warehouse clubs, and supercenters, and sales at the twenty largest food retailers accounted for 65 percent of all sales.[20] Since 2012, food sales have been increasingly concentrated among a handful of supermarkets (e.g.,

Walmart, Kroger, Albertsons, and Target) and 75 percent of households' calories come from supermarkets.[21] Most conventional supermarkets carry a limited range of local produce and meats, which means that most consumers do not have easy access to it.[22] Local foods tend to be slightly more expensive than conventionally grown produce (roughly 15–20 percent more expensive) and according to a 2015 USDA study, consumers do not want to spend the extra money or time to shop at multiple places (e.g., farmers' market, farm stand, or specialty market) for their food.[23] In short, the conventional food system—which is designed to promote food produced at industrial farms that is sold at conventional supermarkets in which low prices and ease of access are prioritized—places local food producers at a significant competitive disadvantage.

At the end of the day, local food producers in central New York face challenges with reaching a public willing and financially able to afford the higher costs for the produce as well as limited access to wholesale and institutional buyers. Although their unwavering commitment to sustainability and stewardship, honesty and transparency helps them develop a market, they are of limited value in helping them address these more intractable challenges. Farmers' moral commitments seem to provide some degree of solace and encourage them to continue their work even in light of hard-to-solve market problems. Jamie Rollins of White Oak Farm captured, in part, how the human-centered aspect of the good farmer ethos keeps her going:

> I continue to do it because it's such meaningful work, it's such important work.... We're helping people to be better people by having better nutrition, and we get to be outside, we get to work with the land, we get to—I mean, it might be one of the only jobs I can think of that feels like entirely good for people. Do you know what I mean? In terms of what we're producing. But vegetables are pretty hands-down good for you.

Overall, I have tried to show how farmers draw on their moral codes to help them create a more stable and predictable environment and to create a different kind of market. Adhering to the codes around sustainability and stewardship allows them to grow high-quality meats and produce that are superior to what is available in supermarkets or through wholesalers who supply restaurants. At the same time, by imbuing food with non-economic meanings and cultivating relationships or at least significant connections between farmer and consumer, they offer additional reasons to purchase their wares. Finally, they draw on a set of interactional norms that promote solidarity and cooperation among local food producers and reduce the uncertainties they face. In the final chapter, I continue the discussion of the challenges facing local food producers but focus on how they were affected by and responded to the COVID-19 pandemic, and then move toward a broader discussion about the future of local food in central New York. The chapter concludes with a review about my findings regarding the relationship between morality, emotions, and local agriculture.

4

Morality, Emotions, and the Future of Local Food

Dan Nowak is a second-generation farmer who successfully made a switch from growing cereal grains on roughly a thousand acres to primarily growing garlic for restaurants on a much smaller plot of land. However, the global pandemic changed everything. The story he told of his entrance into the garlic market and his exit due to the COVID-19 pandemic highlights how a moral code shaped his business model and farming practices; his story also illustrates the precariousness of specialty farming at the local level. After selling a sizeable portion of the farm to a dairy, Dan decided to concentrate on growing vegetables that had more flavor than the industrialized, easily transported produce commonly sold in America's grocery stores. Flavor and preserving old varieties of vegetables featured prominently in his account. He began by jokingly noting that all he wanted for his birthday was "one good peach. When the peaches turned into plastic peaches, I wanted one good peach. I also wanted a good tomato, good vegetables. So I decided to shift over to the way they were when I was a child and start growing them that way. I prefer to go back to the flavors we used to know." He turned to the farming knowledge and skills he inherited from his father, augmented by his strong interest in the science of agronomy and a drive to return to and preserve the crops that have flavor rather than a long shelf life. He began by growing perhaps the tastiest sweet corn in central New York from seed he bred himself. But he also grew hops, which his father had started growing in the late 1920s, as well as a heritage potato that is the precursor to the widely grown Russet Burbank. He doesn't grow a lot of potatoes or hops, especially since a glutted hop market has driven down prices to the extent that he loses money trying to sell them. When I asked why he keeps the hops and potatoes, he voiced his commitment to stewardship and preserving biodiversity:

> They're not prolific potatoes, they grow very few. But since you can't get them anyplace else now, we feel kind of obligated to grow a half a dozen plants every year. Just to make certain that we don't lose the DNA. Because in the end it's diversity that we're all longing for, it's something—biologic and genetic diversity, if it's gone it's gone. So we don't want that to happen. That's why I continue to grow these hops.

His decision to grow garlic was not planned but happened by chance. Friends of a family of local restauranteurs introduced him to the garlic their grandparents brought to America when they immigrated and had kept growing for decades. He was astonished at the taste of the garlic and how much better it was than any garlic he could buy in the supermarket. In 1997 he partnered with one of the family members to grow their garlic and named it in honor of the family's grandfather. His breakthrough into the lucrative New York City restaurant trade came unexpectedly while attending a "foodie" dinner in the Hudson Valley to which a close friend had dragged him. The dinner was billed as "locavore farmer meets gourmet diner." He was invited to bring some of his produce to sell as part of a fundraiser to help the Rockefeller Estate put up a new greenhouse. As they ate, the dinner turned into something out of a Hollywood movie:

> They ran out of garlic in the kitchen. The cook came out and said, "I heard that there was somebody here with some garlic." And we were asked to bring our fine china. Everybody had to bring their own silverware and things to the meal. So we brought our place setting, and for me—we're not fine china people—for a farmer, fine china is the Chinet versus a paper plate when you're eating outdoors. So it wasn't the plate that I was trying to tout, so I put some garlic around my plate as a conversation piece, is really what it was—a conversation starter. And when the chef came

out of the kitchen, and said, "I heard that there was somebody here that has garlic, that saves us from running downtown for some garlic." And I just looked and I said, "Go ahead, take it. Take it all. Fine. Just take it." I figured you spend $360 to eat there you may as well have it all. So he took it and twenty minutes later he came out. "Where did you get that garlic?" A hundred questions. And I said, "No, we're growing this." And he put his hand on my shoulder and he bent down by my ear and he said, "We need to talk." So that's how that got started.

Dan established a long-running partnership with the chef and a few other prominent New York City restaurants that were willing to pay a premium price for his garlic. Those relationships allowed his garlic business to flourish for the next two decades; however, those partnerships floundered when COVID-19 closed restaurants. Few could or would buy his garlic. During a Zoom call in February 2021, he flatly stated, "I am one of the guys going out of business. I'm not going out because I want to but because the restaurants have dropped me." He struggled to get the 2020 crop in because his source of local labor (teenagers who lived in the area) would not work, and when he spoke with the restaurants, "none of them were buying." Although he was able to sell a small amount of seed stock (small cloves of garlic used to establish a garlic patch) to a few farmers (one of whom started a CSA to meet demand for local produce in the Hudson Valley) and artisanal food producers, he gave most of the garlic to a nearby food pantry. As we talked about his future plans, it became clear that his commitment to preserving heritage produce remained, but he saw no avenue forward to return to providing garlic to fine dining restaurants in the city. He offered to teach two different young men to take over the business, but both backed out. Despite ways in which COVID-19 devastated his business, he was not at all bitter. He recognized the legitimacy of restaurant economics: "Because their rent isn't changing, and because a lot of their fixed costs did not budge, their variable costs became critical to them. Why should you spend ten or eleven dollars a pound for garlic when you can buy it for two? Yes, it doesn't have the same flavor, but a good chef can take sow's ear and turn it into a silk purse."

Near the end of the interview, he offered a comment, not with an air of resignation but with a sense of having lived a worthy farming life, one in which he stayed true to his commitments to preserving heritage stock and stewarding the land:

> I'm close enough to the time when I'd have to give this up anyway. I can't be doing this for forty more years, there's no way. I could do it for maybe another decade or two if I'm really lucky, and if I get some help to do things.... I have to keep my seed alive; so that's what I'm going to do now is grow seed for one of my Hudson Valley growers. Just enough to make sure that I can keep them going, keep the seed stock around, and then try to find a place for them.

Throughout my three interviews with Dan, two things stood out: first, his determination to take care of his land and the crops he grew; and second, his intention to breed flavor back into produce. Both stem from the larger moral code he follows (as described in chapter 3), and they also underscore the fundamentally moral nature of food. His life's work communicates a clear message about the good, worthwhile, and right: acting as a steward, preserving biodiversity, and growing crops that are healthy, safe, and flavorful. Moreover, his approach to local agriculture, particularly his partnerships with important tastemakers in the American food scene, suggests that it can transform how we eat because it may reshape the palates of chefs and diners and increase demand for the kind of crops he grows. In her book about heirloom vegetables and fruits, Jennifer Jordan makes a similar claim as she writes about the reciprocal relationship between agricultural landscapes and the markets for food:

> The popularity of McDonald's means a landscape scattered not only with golden arches but also with vast fields of genetically modified corn and

soy. On the other hand, the tastes of a handful of restaurant owners (and their patrons) in California leads to fields of organic Italian greens alive with bees and other fauna and flora.... The growing popularity of heirlooms and other unusual or traditional foods creates further demand, and the landscapes change to meet that demand.[1]

Jordan and I see the potential of local food, but realizing that promise is far more difficult, as intimated by the closing of Dan Nowak's farm. In the next two sections of this final chapter, I first report on my interviewees' hopes for and assessments of its future, and then discuss the present and potential effects of the global pandemic on the local food system in central New York and how the pandemic influenced their hopes or plans for the future. The final section of the chapter takes a theoretical turn as I reflect on the research's lessons about emotions and moral action.

Pre-Pandemic Assessments of Local Food

Near the end of my interviews, I asked each participant to offer their assessment of the current state of the local food system and their assessment of what the future might hold. No matter what role they played in the system or how long they had been involved, their answers almost always identified the progress that had been made over the past decade as well as the limits on growth. They spoke in the tenor of optimism, but it was tempered by uncertainty and worry. Most commonly, chefs and those who run CSAs or farmers' markets spoke about the "low-hanging fruit" problem. That is, while they lauded the growing interest and participation among the public in purchasing local foods or supporting locavore restaurants, they were concerned that they had reached only the "foodie" or gourmet eaters of the region and that they seemed unable to attract others. Thus, they were unsure whether the local food market could grow, and the chefs were reluctant to more directly try to educate diners (especially those they labeled the "filet medium" crowd who comprise one-third to one-half of their customers).

Andrea Hughes, who manages one of the larger farmers' markets in the region, noted that an increasing number of shoppers are "understanding more and more the seasonality of the food and why you shouldn't wander in looking for strawberries in January. It [i.e., seasonality] also helps them appreciate it when the food is there, and that drives them to support the people growing the food." At the same time, she voiced a concern that there are now too many markets for the relatively small population in the region: "I think it gets to the point, like, all of a sudden having a farmers' market was trendy. You were cutting-edge and you were being farm-to-table and focusing on organic and all. It's not a bad thing. Everybody wants to do it, and then we all kind of stand around and all our vendors say, 'Now we don't have any consumers.'" Several chefs wondered aloud whether the region could support additional farm-to-table restaurants. While we sat in his restaurant, Larry Cooper, who runs Green Gables Eatery, shook his head when I asked him about the prospects of more farm-to-table restaurants opening up. But he thought for a minute or two and then suggested how a creative entrepreneur could succeed:

> If somebody were to open another restaurant, they've got to do something special. There's no more room for just another restaurant. . . . If I was opening a restaurant today I'd make sure I had acreage enough to grow a farm and hire the people and run it in conjunction. It's a farm and it's a restaurant. You can't get any closer. . . . Wouldn't it be cool if you could have a family come out and they pick the vegetables that you're going to prepare for them for dinner, like I pulled those beets, like I said I used to do. Kids don't get to do that anymore. I shelled the peas or picked the peas, or snipped the green beans.

His comments suggest that one path forward might be to combine local food with agritourism and education. This hypothetical restaurant would occupy a new place in the market (as none currently run their own farm) and offer unique sensory experiences that could make the benefits of local food more tangible for unfamiliar diners. By targeting children, it could help socialize a new generation to embrace a locavore diet. Fellow chefs Sam Cook and Thad Russell also mused about the possibility of turning central New York into a locavore destination. They wondered whether the locavore scene could be anchored along the Erie Canal and the foothills of Adirondack Park. Russell wistfully voiced this hope: "It's a long shot, but in fifteen or twenty years it could become a food hub, it could be a place that people travel to because of the bounty of the Adirondacks, right on the southern border of the Adirondacks. We're only ninety miles north of the Finger Lakes, we're centrally located between Albany and Buffalo, and we could draw a lot of the food grown here, and also a lot of the customers and become a destination."

Most of the interviewees agreed that the future of local food depends on meeting three goals: educating the non-locavore public about the benefits of local food (in terms of taste, health/safety, and improving the local economy); developing the infrastructure to improve reliability and accessibility across the entire system; and making local food affordable to lower-income residents. Farmers' market manager Andrea Hughes spoke about the need to help shoppers understand how to cook vegetables with which they are not familiar and mused about the possibility of offering cooking classes each week at her market. More importantly, she identified a larger concern about the need to change the "mindset" of the public. She suggested that they need to not only think about food in terms of eating in-season but also revalue food so that they are "not just looking for the best deal, the cheapest product, what you can throw in a microwave at the end of a long day." Scott Ingalls, the executive chef at Union Park Café who first voiced his frustration that his best seller is the beef filet entrée that his local farmers cannot fully supply, then spoke about the need to change how diners calculate the value of the meals he offers and more generally of local food:

> It really is a lot of education. Because otherwise, let me summarize that by saying, the phrase that we talk about a lot in staff is "value." Somewhere

along the way the word "value" came to mean, like, "bargain," right? That's not what value is. Value is, did you get what you paid for? A Mercedes-Benz is a good value. Or Doc Martens are a good value. Or Patagonia is a good value. If you paid good money for something and it lasted you a long time, that's a good value. If you paid good money for a meal and you left satiated and pleasantly satisfied, then you got a good value. A good value is not getting a good deal. That's a bargain. Are we a bargain? No, we're not a bargain, hell no! And that's what this is about to me—if you charge more, did you live up to it? Was the quality of the product the best you could find? Did you work as hard as you could not to screw it up? Did you train your employees to know everything that they could to guide the guest through that more expensive experience? And in the end, did the guest smile at you and tell you that they had a good time, and maybe leave a nice review and a good gratuity? That's a good value.

Karen Williams, who manages a different farmers' market, focuses her educational work on children, with an eye toward developing lifelong dietary habits and socializing younger generations to appreciate and desire local food. She participates in a national program to teach kids about healthy foods. Each market day, kids are offered two dollars in tokens that they can spend at any of the farmers' booths. She reported that the experience of purchasing fruits and vegetables and talking to farmers "teaches kids at a very young age to make that healthy choice instead of lemonade because they can only use the tokens on fruit and vegetables." Unfortunately, Karen had no data to suggest that this educational work is effective, at least not in the short term. Such strategies suggest that expanding the pool of locavore consumers may be a long and slow process.

Several chefs believe that a heavy-handed educational effort simply will alienate those who are not already on the local food bandwagon, as discussed in chapter 3. Sam Cook of the Leatherstocking Inn made this point most explicitly when I asked him about the future of local food in the region:

You know, the whole population in general, it moves slowly. And it's just gonna go with the culture. You can't beat it into people, you have to just kind of slowly expose them to that. And it's happening because when they go to the stores, they see it at the stores. . . . I mean, you can go to one of the big chain grocery stores at this time of year and you walk in and they'll have a sign that says, these zucchinis are from this farm outside of Syracuse. People—for a long time I don't think people really connected that their food comes from a farm. They don't really get the idea of, like, you show someone a brussels sprout stalk and they go, what the heck is that? Well, that's a brussels sprout! People have no idea. So when you show them, when they see that stuff in the markets and then they see it again in a restaurant, it helps.

Greg Rose, an organic beef farmer, offered a different perspective on education around local food insofar as he argued that the farmer needs to learn how to run their business differently:

I'm also fully convinced that most farmers would be better off serving a wholesale market and concentrating on a few things that they can do very well. I think that that's the future rather than trying to develop their own retail. There could be some exceptions. There's probably still room for some local farm stands that could be supplied by one farm and do okay. But the whole farmers' market circuit thing is, that's a very limited approach. . . . Most farmers still have more of the mindset of figuring out how to market what they want to grow. I think that is a backwards approach from what I would recommend for a farmer. Rather than figuring out how to market what you want to grow, figure out how to grow what they want to buy.

In short, most producers believe that educating the public about the benefits of local produce, meats, and prepared foods is a critical step toward expanding the size of the market, but alone it has limited value. One of the drawbacks of most local food systems, including the one in central New York, is that the infrastructure to distribute it and to make consumer purchases easier is not very well developed. By infrastructure I refer to the processing, storage, distribution, and retail operations that can serve both wholesale and retail buyers.[2] Practically this may take the shape of food cooperatives, or other local food retail outlets, farmers' markets, or food hubs.[3] The infrastructure in central New York is rudimentary—several farmers' markets, a small number of meat processors, one vegetable processor that serves wholesale markets, one nonprofit that helps individuals develop, market, and meet food safety regulations for value-added food products such as barbeque sauce or jam, and three health food stores that carry some local dairy and produce.[4] The largest farmers' markets and health food stores are clustered around a few small cities and therefore are not easily accessible to all farmers or consumers in the region. Moreover, during the data collection period, two small food hubs that operated out of Syracuse closed, as did two local food stores. Several of the health food stores in central New York carry a limited range of local meats, dairy, and produce, but it constitutes roughly 5–10 percent of their entire inventory. When I asked the owner of Harvest Moon Health Foods, one of the larger health and organic food stores in the region, he spoke at length about the challenges he faced getting farmers to commit a portion of their crops to his store:

> I feel a real struggle with the local produce people, and I'm not totally faulting them, but I think they really don't want to deal with me, they want to just deal with the farmers' markets. And it's not that I don't want to deal with them, they don't even reach out to me. Over the years, I always would buy it if the opportunity's there, but I'm not gonna go begging somebody. . . . I've bought, like, maybe not this year or the year before, but I've had produce people come in and they're all gung ho, blah blah blah, and they saw me once or twice. And I pay them to bring it in, so it's not like I'm not paying them. And then they disappear. And I think the problem is limited growing season, limited amount of what

they can grow, and I think they're able to move all through the CSAs and the farmers' markets.

At the same time, the dozens of companies with whom he has contracts tend to only offer national-brand organic foods. There is no local or regional distributor who can supply him with local fruits, vegetables, meat, eggs, or dairy, and thus he is left to establish relationships with individual producers, which, as he noted, may not happen at all or may happen for only one or two growing seasons. In short, the lack of wholesalers and farmers' preference to use farmers' markets (i.e., the existing infrastructure) make it difficult for him reliably to keep local products on his shelves. In response, farmers have begun to develop alternative direct-to-consumer marketing practices. Several operate farm stands where they carry other farmers' meats, cheeses, or processed foods (e.g., jams) and they created an online ordering system where customers may pick up produce, meats, and cheeses when the farmers' markets are not operating. Some farmers rent refrigerator/freezer space at small grocery stores for their meats and cheeses to expand the reach of their market. While such practices may bolster sales for individual farmers, this ad hoc and piecemeal approach does not address larger systemic infrastructural problems.

Several chefs also voiced concerns about the lack of infrastructure. While chefs try to establish long-standing relationships with different farmers, even starting restaurant-supported agriculture type agreements (RSAs), they still face the logistical challenge of keeping track of multiple, sometimes dozens, of contracts and relationships with various meat, dairy, and vegetable producers, rather than getting the majority of their ingredients from one vendor. Thad Russell from City Diner summed up the prospect of a local food hub and more generally the vision of a well-developed local food distribution system:

> I think it would make our jobs a little bit easier, because we would be able to discover new things, we'd be able to see—like, you were talking about

farmers' markets, if there was a hub, if you will, kind of like, hopefully the Locavore [a new store that primarily stocked local vegetables and meats a few miles from his restaurant] takes off to the point where we can go in there and if we only need five pounds of heirloom carrots, and they have that from a local farmer, we don't have to go out of our way and have an order minimum with somebody that needs to have two or three hundred dollars in order to deliver it to us. If we could just go pick that up and have that kind of responsible feeling that, we just bought local, that would be fantastic. So yes, with the Locavore opening up soon, and if we had more than that, if we had a year-round farmers' market, maybe even indoors, that would be just incredible.

The Locavore closed its doors within two years of opening, in part due to its inconvenient location, in part due to its reliance on word-of-mouth advertising, and in part due to the high costs of its wares, all of which inhibited sales. The extra costs associated with selling via a middle person (for farmers, selling at their own farm stand or through online sales may be more profitable options) and the inconvenience for shoppers suggest that simply building the infrastructure for local food is not a panacea. Paul Weber, who turned toward institutional sales when he could barely break even with various CSA business models, captured the convenience dilemma facing local food producers:

I think there's a relatively small group of people, the low-hanging fruit, that have the time and ability and financial wherewithal to shop from farms. Because at the end of the day it's not convenient. CSAs are not as convenient as the other options. Our farm store was more convenient than CSAs but still not as convenient as a grocery store. So I think there's this small group that's going to go out of their way and has the ability to go out of their way. I think there's a much larger group of people that would be just as happy to get local food, if not more happy, to get local food, but it's not the priority for them. It's not the thing that they're willing to go out of their way for. . . . I think if you could make local food just as successful and convenient as what most people are buying, then I think people would be really happy to buy local food.

His comments suggest that the market for local foods is organized by income level and a willingness to seek out local meats and produce that often are located away from population centers. In other words, the growth or expansion of local food may be limited by the resources available to consumers as well as by the lack of infrastructure to make purchases convenient. He continued talking about the future of local food by recognizing the financial challenges with its higher costs than supermarket foods and how this limits potential growth of the market.

> We're certainly going to be more expensive. Local farmers just can't afford to be as cheap as some other options, and I understand why people don't want to spend that money for food, or don't feel that they can.... It seems to me so wrapped up in all these other big problems, you know, income inequality and things like that, that I don't think anything big and radical is going to happen without other big radical things happening.

In this final statement, Paul identifies one of the most important barriers to expanding the reach of local food. Farmers and other actors cannot afford to sell their food more cheaply, but a significant part of the population in central New York does not have the financial means to purchase the food. It is certainly beyond the ability of farmers, many of whom are struggling financially, to address systemic inequality. Yet several are aware of the inequities built into the food system, raised concerns about food security or food justice during our interviews, and identified their small efforts to address them. For example, toward the end of our conversation with Melissa Harrison of Hidden Hills CSA about the future of her farm and more generally local food in central New York, she raised this issue. She expressed her hope that her farm and others could do more to serve lower-income and non-white customers in the region. Not only would this be a key to growth for the system, but also it would help make the community more just. In her comments, she criticized the classed and raced nature of local food in the area and in the United States, and introduced a new justice orientation as part of the moral code that guides her work. She mentioned that they have started offering reduced-cost subscriptions to refugees and low-income residents in the county and have been actively working with community activists in a nearby city to connect the farm with communities of color.

> So what is happening there is more interesting to me, and culturally, the disconnect, especially with communities of color and low income. I mean, obviously the whole economy is so broken and stacked against poor people and stacked against farms and the food system. It's really hard, but I'm very curious about that connection and what creative solutions can happen there. Because the more I've learned, the more I've gotten to know people in communities of color. First of all they love coming to the farm, they love being in the country, they don't have opportunities to be here and don't feel welcome here—and secondly, they want fresh fruit. So the desire is there. . . . What I would love to see, and I don't know if this will happen or I don't know how to make this happen, is to break out of that predictable path and say we don't need it to just be the Prius-driving liberals. And what can all of us do—sociology professors, farmers, and the average consumer, all of us do to break down the segregation that is so taken for granted? We take for granted that we know nothing about the people in our poorer communities, and they know nothing about us. It's such a segregated American life. And I would love to participate in breaking that segregation and realizing that this local food thing doesn't have to be a white middle-class kind of a niche. How we get there I don't know, but it seems like if we put our intention there, there will be some progress.

Melissa Harrison's ideal market it one that is inclusive and accessible to everyone in the community (not just, she noted, the white middle-class population) and it aims to focus the market around justice more than profit. Food justice "is the struggle against racism, exploitation, oppression taking place within the food system that addresses inequality's root causes both within and beyond the food chain."[5] Yet the small size of her farm, the limits to growth on which she operates, and the challenges of connecting low-income residents with the farm in a region with poor public transportation will make it difficult to realize this kind of market. Moreover, the scale, depth, and intractability of income inequality and poverty mean that they require public policy and legal solutions, as well as creative economic restructuring in the region that can turn an aging rustbelt region into one with well-paying jobs that will give residents the financial wherewithal to afford local food and even expand the population of the region, which in turn could expand the pool of local food consumers. Although the local food system appeared stable and most participants were guardedly optimistic about the future, the arrival of the COVID-19 pandemic created new challenges, increased market uncertainty, and in some cases, threatened to shut down significant parts of the system.

The Challenges and Opportunities Posed by COVID-19

As soon as the United States and the rest of the world went into lockdown in order to limit the spread of the COVID-19 virus, the media began reporting on its effect on the global food system. Restaurants shuttered and laid off employees; grocery stores ran out of essential food items such as flour; dairy farmers were dumping thousands of gallons of milk because they couldn't get it to milk co-ops; crops rotted in fields; and bottlenecks in supply lines developed as consumer demands changed. For example, a story from a Minnesota newspaper noted how "a Minnesota cheese producer donated 18,000 pounds of product after an indoor dining shutdown caused a backlog of supply," thus losing a significant part of their income stream. The reporter also wrote about how changes in demand for meat, a shortage of freezers, and too few workers at meat processors adversely affected meat production:

Local meat producers have faced a unique snag in the production cycle. Part of the problem is created by changes in demand, said Colleen Carlson, an educator at the University of Minnesota Extension who works closely with Scott and Carver counties. But an unexpected challenge has been a shortage of freezers, Carlson said, which are an integral part of the preservation and transport process. . . . On top of a shortage of individual freezers for local meat producers, the demand for local locker plants has skyrocketed, creating a bottleneck effect on the production process, which takes several days and has been slowed down by the current supply chain, Carlson said. Processing plants, too, have had to reconsider how much product they take in. Carlson says some are currently running at only 60–80% capacity.[6]

As the pandemic stretched into months, we began to hear more encouraging news about rising demand for CSA subscriptions, stories about how some restaurants were shifting to takeout and/or setting up feeding programs for essential workers, and accounts of how farmers' markets adopted new COVID-19 protocols to stay safely open. For example, some National Public Radio stories reported that demand for CSA subscriptions was outpacing the ability of farmers to meet it, while others shifted their business from supplying restaurants to running CSAs or farm stands.[7] The crucial issue facing local farmers and other producers is whether or not this change in demand for local food is short-term or signals a fundamental change in how Americans eat. Both worried and curious about how my interviewees were affected by the pandemic, I sent emails to them inquiring about how they were coping with all of the changes or challenges posed by COVID-19. Nick Constantino, who helps the region's farmers develop their business models and has his pulse on the agricultural community, summarized the overall effects of COVID-19 on the agricultural system in central New York:

All our nursery people and flowers and cut hay had the best year of their life. The farm stands had a banner year. Demand for local meat exploded.

People were buying chest freezers and buying quarters and halves of livestock and pork. And that absolutely exploded, which then caused the livestock processing places to get super busy. . . . Your vegetable people had a tremendous year, but your fluid milk and dairy were tremendously negatively impacted. . . . The direct farm market people did well. Now if your target audience was restaurants, you got killed. Obviously, the restaurants took the biggest hit of everybody.

In general, local food producers were wary but hopeful prior to the pandemic, and now they are more nervous and unsure whether the work they did to stay afloat will be enough in the coming years. "Cautious" was the most common word interviewees used to describe their hopes for the future amidst the pandemic. The closing paragraph of Thad Russell's email aptly summarizes the challenges, opportunities, and wary optimism he and his peers voiced in response to my email query:

The shutdown from the pandemic was certainly unexpected, as was the length of time we were closed. It has challenged us to reassess our business and create new sources of revenue, our ability to source unique and specialty produce, and the farmers and producers we work with directly. It has also impacted our staffing and turnover, forcing some to question working in the industry. Overall, it has been a year of changes, reflection and evaluation. We are hopeful that we will continue to grow and change to maintain ourselves as a viable business and continue to support our local economy.

In short, the pandemic's effects were uneven. Farmers who sold directly to consumers were in good shape, but those whose primary clients were restaurants or wholesalers struggled. Nearly one-third of my interviewees responded to my email request, and all but two of their responses fell into one of three categories: serious hardship; initial hardship but then good fortune following adaptation of their business; or limited effect. Two farms who did not conform to the patterns reported unexpected and rather phenomenal success from direct market sales. Their responses suggest that advanced planning and an ability to change direction quickly were keys to their success. Sarah Wilson, whose Twin Ponds Farm specializes in meat, had sold out her entire spring supply by April. By following her usual practice of placing her meat processing order in January, she had all of her meat in her freezers when COVID-19 created the rush in early and late spring. She wrote, "Good thing I did because butchers were booked up for the year really fast—this never happens by the way. I listed on our online store when we had bulk orders available and the amount, people made their choices and paid a deposit. By the end of April, we had reservations on about 90% of our meats." She also expanded her garden and sold produce at an open-air farm stand for much of the summer. She reported that they had a steady stream of customers at the farm during the season, and by carefully watching their expenses, they actually saw a sizeable increase in profits. The owner of Wilson Farm also reported that the pandemic year was his most profitable ever. At the onset of the pandemic, he turned his farm stand into an agritourist destination for the region. He saw the demand for an outdoor place to which families could escape and be safe. He created mazes in his corn and sunflower fields, offered hay rides, more u-pick options, and live music at a new bandstand. While produce sales were down by 50 percent (due to slow sales at farmers' markets and a summer drought), the agritourism business grew by 900 percent over 2019. The profit allowed him to buy new equipment, install a green energy heating system, and upgrade his buildings and parking lot, all of which he hopes will help him continue this amazing reversal of fortune. At the end of the note he sent me, he offered the following analysis about how the necessity of foresight, risk taking, and flexibility saved his farm:

> 2020 turned out to be the biggest year ever for us in sales, expansions and positive turn around but only because I did it by the numbers and understand what needed to be done to remain ahead of the curve thrown our way. Businesses that failed did so because they could not change fast

enough or allowed themselves to fail without taking risks and understanding what was at hand. Yes, I am nervous about this year but continue to expand and adjust as needed based upon last year's numbers. We gave the public normalcy and a safe environment to do so.

These two farms were the exception. Most of the farmers who responded to my email inquiry reported either that they experienced significant challenges or at best were only marginally affected. The CSAs who participated in the study appear to have been the least adversely affected by the pandemic. Most noticed an increase in requests to join, but only one of the four who responded to my email, Red Maple Farm, expanded in a significant manner. The other three faced limits on how much land they could place under cultivation, and neither Harmony Farm nor Hidden Hills was interested in expanding. Melissa Harrison, owner of the latter, wrote that she saw the communal nature of her CSA blossoming as a large number of members sought out the farm as a "refuge":

> We noticed that our farm has been especially sought out as a refuge for individuals, families and children, who want to be outside together. Whether picking herbs and flowers, chasing the chickens, pressing apple cider, honoring solstice, harvesting garlic, sharing hearts and minds around a fire, making plant medicine, praying in a women's church group, practicing yoga or attending a racism workshop, many more people found our farm to be an oasis this year. This is a primary goal of ours.

Her summary suggests that the community formation goals for her CSA, which were almost a second thought for most of her members, became much more important during the pandemic. As well, the pandemic may have served as an impetus for Melissa to do more (such as setting up weekly yoga classes and sending out regular reminders to her members that the farm was open 24/7 for them to visit) to help foment community. Several other interviewees commented about how the pandemic seemed to trigger a yearning among the public for community and connections.

Sarah Wilson of Twin Ponds Farm reported that consumers "flocked" to their farm stand during the year. Ed Peters, who grows garlic, beef, and lamb at Lucky Acres Farm, captured the community-engagement effect of the pandemic eloquently:

> The pandemic has trapped people in their homes and taking a ride in the country in 2020 was equivalent to taking a ride in the country in the 1950's. The average Joes, men covered in tattoos, men in suits, women in booty shorts, women that are high steppers, girls in tie-dyed shirts and beads around their neck—all walks of life came to the farm and you could feel their smiles through their masks just to be out of the coffins of their homes and happily sharing a conversation with someone new (me). I know in the media 2020 was a horrible time, a horrible leader, horrible treatment to minorities, and America was a place that the media showed being almost equally divided. That was NOT [emphasis original] my first-hand experience, I saw the pandemic bring all walks of life together and people helping one another and the focus on the family once again being the hearth. Perhaps the children and father didn't split the wood, but the kitchen became the focal point of the home. Families ate at home, prepared meals together, and talk with one another at dinner, like I did as a child with my family.

A second group of producers reported that they struggled initially both financially and practically during the early months of the pandemic, but in the end emerged from the first year exhausted but feeling stable. Many of those who weathered the challenges posed by the pandemic did so because they were able to adapt their business models. The managers of three different farmers' markets reported that sales were modestly down and their markets were not as busy as usual, which they attributed to strict social distancing protocols and mask mandates. However, they and their vendors switched to use online ordering systems, and by the end of the first summer seemed to have recovered. One wrote about how farmers, like many Americans, were divided about just how serious the pandemic was, and those who didn't believe that it was serious tended to face greater financial struggles:

> If a farm was selling direct to consumer and had dismal sales it is likely because they would not make adjustments to meet consumer demand. Sad, but that's what I saw. I even tried to assist some of them but too many times it was ignored. So many people just couldn't grasp the seriousness or long-term impact of a pandemic. We had farmers who just told me that the farmers market didn't need to make changes.

The cheesemakers at High Meadow Dairy found themselves dumping milk for several days, but then quickly pivoted to a new plan that involved bottling their own milk. Barbara Allen relayed how the addition of a bottling operation was aided by a bit of good media coverage because it helped build support within the community. They also joined with other farms by forming a cooperative farm store in order to expand the reach to a wider pool of consumers:

> The day that we were to send our first shipment, the demand for milk had plummeted to a point where our cooperative could not find a market to sell milk. We ended up dumping milk for several days. We immediately looked into what it would take to bottle our own milk. We called our inspectors and found equipment that we rented and eventually purchased. We started bottling milk in April. The local news station heard about us and did a news story about our situation. We ended up having lines of people coming to purchase our farm fresh milk immediately after our story aired. We have continued the milk production along with our cheese and increased our business during these tumultuous times.... The creamery business has definitely contributed to the farm's success this past year. We have gained a steady local business and have high hopes of keeping these customers as the trends toward buying from local small business rise. We have also worked in conjunction with other local farms selling each other's products in hope to lift us all up.

The widely shared ethos of cooperation, creativity, and some help from friends seemed to be the key ingredients that turned disaster into survival and even profit. One of the most telling accounts was provided by the owner of Three Willows Farm, Theresa Mahoney. The farm, which specializes in a variety of cheeses, gelatos, and meats, had just began a $200,000 addition to their cheese plant, which was financed mainly through mortgaging their home, when the pandemic hit. "We lost nearly 95% of our sales in less than a week. I called everyone we owed money to and told them we wouldn't be able to pay our bills. I was genuinely panicked. . . . At one point I traded eggs for toilet paper." The sudden loss of income occurred because the largest share of their food was sold to restaurants, which had shut down. But then members of the community began to show up at the farm looking to buy food. One of the chefs with whom they worked took YouTube viewers on a tour of the farm and made a plea for central New Yorkers to support Three Willows and other local farmers. Within several weeks Theresa and her husband redirected their business to retail and on-farm sales. They applied for PPP (Paycheck Protection Program) and SBA (Small Business Administration) loans to give them the working capital to pay bills, complete the new cheese plant, and set up their retail operation. She explained that it was not easy and she is not sure whether they will make it through the pandemic, but they have come through it so far with their farm and livelihood intact:

> It was the combination of all these strange factors that made me realize that people still needed to eat and we just needed to pivot our business to reach them. Since then, we've done everything we can to respond to customer needs. We take online orders for pickup, shipping or delivery. We opened a small store in our new cheese plant and filled it with our goods and products from other farmer friends. We are currently working with a group of farmers to host a "Farmer's Pack-It," where customers place their orders ahead of time & pick them up at one central location. . . . So, in a nutshell, we are doing well, but thoroughly exhausted. We have virtual

whiplash from all the pivoting, and are only cautiously optimistic about the future. We take one day at time.

The accounts of the farmers in my study and how they quickly adjusted to new demands and new opportunities created by the pandemic mirror responses in other states as reported by both scholars and journalists. For example, a recent study of Vermont's local and regional food systems found that many farmers rapidly pivoted to build greater ability to sell directly to consumers as restaurant sales plummeted.[8]

My interviewees' statements about how they coped with the challenges of the pandemic highlight how strong emotions—in this case, fear, worry, and discouragement—triggered creative responses. At the same time, their adaptive responses hinged on mobilizing members of their farm networks and communities, calling on a shared ethos of cooperation, and quickly figuring out how to shift resources and their work practices to meet and/or generate new consumer demand. A friend who farms near my college reminded me as we talked over this chapter that farmers are accustomed to and often ready to cope with disasters that threaten their crops and livelihoods. He suggested that the ability to pivot quickly is part of the farming mindset, which may have helped them respond and in some cases thrive as the pandemic continued. They also had some time to adjust as the pandemic hit before many crops were in the field. The restaurants in the study did not have the luxury of time to develop their responses, nor was it as easy to change how to run a restaurant when dining in was not allowed for months and when local food was not always available to them.

Although all of the restaurants in the study that were open at the start of 2020 are still open, they struggled more than any other group. The chefs at City Diner and Union Park reported revenue losses upwards of 50 percent from the prior year. PPP funding and SBA loans allowed them to retain some of their workforce. Both shifted to takeout but with a limited menu and at greatly reduced hours than their restaurants operated at before the pandemic. In addition, City Diner prepared lunches for first responders for several months, which were often paid for by donations from members of the community as well as a few special takeout dinners. Union Park hosted a series of virtual dinners in which the chefs would create the dishes for delivery or curbside pickup, and then from 6:00 to 9:00 p.m. would walk diners through reheating and plating the meals, talk about the food and wine pairings, and field questions. Although these dinners were very successful and kept the kitchen staff working, they were of limited financial value to the restaurant. According to Thad Russell of City Diner, the ways in which they responded to the pandemic primarily served an important symbolic purpose and helped boost the morale of the staff and the community:

> We launched a "Feed the Frontline" campaign and partnered with hospitals and local organizers to get pre-packaged meals to hospital, nursing home, and other healthcare staff. We asked patrons to purchase gift cards, and we then used the funds to cover $10 meals that were individually packaged and delivered to their destination. We were able to secure revenue while providing a thanks to those working tirelessly to keep us safe. We also created a "Date Night for Two Dinner" so our patrons could enjoy a full meal, complete with wine and dessert, at home while our dining room was closed. For Thanksgiving and Christmas holidays, we created family meals, which allowed us to prepare special holiday meals and send them ready to serve or with limited preparation at home. While none of these new avenues replaced our lost revenue, they allowed us to maintain a steady source of sales. I can confidently say that none of these items would have had a market pre-pandemic. However, we wanted to do our part to maintain a sense of normalcy, reduce stress, and provide a great meal for others.

The efforts of both restaurants align with their goals of promoting community and following an ethic of care and hospitality. Thad Russell's detailed response to my inquiry also reveals how the farm-restaurant community began to break down even as new relationships emerged

MORALITY, EMOTIONS, AND THE FUTURE OF LOCAL FOOD | 149

as the region moved out of lockdown. I reprint a substantial part of his email in order to fully capture the ways in which the local food chain was profoundly challenged and reshaped by COVID-19 as well as to highlight how his moral code continued to guide the business:

> Many of the small family growers we purchased from in 2019 did not plant for 2020, and I would not be surprised to hear if some skip the 2021 season. From my conversations with many of them, I gleaned that the costs of the seeds (especially the heirloom and rare varieties restaurants like ours prize) are very high and without a strong market in which to sell their produce, they could not take the financial risk. Many farmers will grow a specific amount of specialty produce for farm to table restaurants under contract which allows the restaurant to have a steady supply of crops and the farmer a guaranteed profit margin. Many of these specialty items would otherwise be too costly to produce. With the loss of revenue and uncertainty regarding our capacity, we made the difficult decision to steer away from some of the most expensive local products in order to cut our COGS [cost of goods sold] by 4–5%, which was necessary for our survival.
>
> Additionally, the pandemic affected some producers in unexpected and unanticipated ways. Due to the strong interest in "homesteading" because of the pandemic, some of our producers found it much more difficult to source needed items for productions. A particular example was when a local chicken producer explained to us that there was "a run on chicks." They had to source chicks through small orders with multiple suppliers, rather than a single supplier they had used for years prior. These farmers also had amazing interest in their products, fueled by support for locally sourced meats and produce. They completely sold out of their supply of whole chickens in days.
>
> While we have lost many small local farmers, our ability to remain committed to the local food economy was not affected due to the strong emergence of two new regional food hubs. These co-ops helped allow us to order smaller amounts of many different items from many different

producers while giving the producers a centralized place to bring their goods to a larger market.

Chef Russell's analysis illustrates several insights about the nature of local food in central New York. First, he identified how changes in demand and supply cascaded across the entire local food system and revealed its precariousness. As farmers shifted production from institutions to individual consumers, and as some chose to not plant specialty crops (e.g., microgreens), particular food items were no longer available for restaurants, which required chefs to alter their menus and made it more difficult to maintain their locavore identity. Second, his comments about the emergence of new distributors, their ability to adapt their menu, and the continued support of patrons speak to the resilience of the system. Third, local food continues to be driven by values despite how pressures to simply survive may have pushed producers to compromise. The City Diner chefs remained committed to sourcing ingredients locally and embodied the ethic of care I discussed in chapter 3. The various ways in which consumers in different communities responded to help farmers and restaurants also reflect a desire to demonstrate concern and care for other members of their communities, and to support the local economy. Finally, it appeared that farmers and chefs moved beyond the initial panic created by the pandemic by simply doing what they know best—farming and cooking. In other words, they drew on their farming or culinary repertoires to guide their adaptive responses and create a sense of normalcy.

Some Provisional Conclusions about the Future of Local Food

Prior to the pandemic, the local food system in central New York was stable and fairly well institutionalized. The CSAs, meat and cheese producers, and a variety of retail outlets (multiple farmers' markets in the counties of the study, health food stores, and farm stands) had developed ongoing relationships with consumers and restaurants. While the overall market was small as most of the participants were committed locavores, it offered producers certainty. However, few producers believed that the market could easily grow unless the pool of consumers could expand to include lower-income groups, persuade consumers to pay the higher prices than those in conventional supermarkets, and develop an agritourism industry that would attract those who live outside central New York. These are not goals that can be met in a short time frame, and several interviewees expect the growth of the system to be slow and perhaps take ten to twenty years. They also believe that growth will depend on the region developing a more robust job market and creative economic initiatives that could make local food more affordable and accessible.

Numerous food scholars have identified significant challenges to the expansion and increased viability of local food systems. In particular they identify scope and scale, and problems with building community that appear to limit the reach and success of local food. Hinrichs and Barham note that too often local food systems are too local and thus farmers, activists, and food professionals may not be aware of or possess the resources to build networks and institutions to connect local systems into larger regional ones.[9] One group of food scholars suggests that local food systems need "weavers," or actors who can build networks and coalitions across agricultural regions and sectors in order to scale up local food:

> Weaver work takes on several tactical orientations. Intrasectoral work forges connections among groups in a given agri-food interest area, such as by organizing producer cooperatives into a federation to strengthen capacity and market position or by maintaining a list serve for a network of CSA farms. Intersectoral linkages connect different agrifood interests and groups with complementary agendas such as by linking farm groups with environmental groups on the issue of farmland preservation or by linking nutritionists with "buy local" campaign organizers.[10]

Additionally, farmers who grow for the local market tend to cultivate small farms and thus can only serve a small population, and, as many of my interviewees explained, wholesalers, processors, and institutional buyers (such as restaurants, school districts, or hospitals) are often not interested in purchasing from small producers. Most of the farmers in this study are not able to expand by adding new acres into production (whether planting additional acres they rented or owned, or buying new land) or pay for new labor if they could expand (and most of the producers rely on themselves or family members for labor). Most do not have extra time to sell at additional farmers' markets (which requires a full day at the market rather than on the farm) or online as they already sell all of what they grow. Clearly no amount of entrepreneurial creativity by the current set of central New York farmers will produce viable long-term solutions. Rather, private and public ventures to enhance collaboration and expand both production and access to local foods seem necessary. This could take the form, for example, of state-level and county-level grants to develop food hubs and new regional processing and distribution organizations, along with incentivizing institutional purchasing of local foods (especially since Americans tend to spend about 55 percent of their household food budgets on eating away from home).[11] Perhaps state and county governments also could recruit new farmers by offering financial help to purchase and/or improve agricultural land, invest in large-scale urban farms, or support the construction of greenhouses so farmers could extend the growing season. Developing economies of scale and improving public transportation so a larger part of the region's population could get to farmers' markets could also make the local food system more viable.

In central New York, practically this might mean formalizing the current ad hoc cooperative efforts of CSA farmers or expanding the food processing infrastructure in the study area to open up new institutional or wholesale markets for farmers. Some of my interviewees believe that the future might rest on the development of a more regional approach. For example, Nick Constantino claimed that the various national and international shortages and bottlenecks in the food system may push producers to create regional systems:

I think things are all going to start to be regionalized, you know, people are going to start to build, like, borders around a region and make sure each region is able to sustain itself. You got a regional dairy processing industry and meat processing industry, a produce processing, you know, they're not going to want to rely on these huge corporations and these huge operations that are thousands of miles away.

The founding of two new regional food co-ops, mentioned by Thad Russell, may bring greater certainty and more options for both individuals and institutional buyers. Many interviewees noted that processing, distribution, and retail infrastructures are critical parts of the food system that need to be developed if it is to continue to grow. The failures of prior food hubs and local food stores over the past five years suggest that keeping the infrastructure viable may be the real challenge that lies ahead.

The second challenge food scholars identify is the ability of local food systems to create a large, committed pool of consumers. One of the promises of local food is that it is intended to build new communities by integrating the farm and non-farm populations such that consumers would willingly shift their food purchases to local farms because they felt so well connected to producers and other locavores. Numerous other food scholars have also found that creating authentic, enduring communities of producers and consumers is not as common as advocates of local food systems promise. Much of the research that investigates claims about the important ways CSAs or other local food institutions create community indicates that this goal is not easily or often met. While consumers and farmers often report the value and importance of the relationships they develop as individuals, few report that shopping at a farmers' market or joining a CSA integrated them into a community.[12]

DeLind argues that the fundamental barrier to building community is that we are so deeply embedded in a transactional and instrumental approach to food that building strong and enduring producer-consumer relationships and developing a local food community are at best secondary goals of participating in the local food system and often simply not part of the consumers' calculus. Moreover, policies and practices to develop local food advanced by activists are built on rational goals about improving access, availability, and visibility. However, they tend to turn local food production and consumption into simple market transactions, and those market relationships may be as transient as the pint of organic strawberries purchased at the farmers' market. She writes,

> Farmers, on the one hand, are being encouraged to developed value-added products, niche markets, and new arrangements for the direct marketing of "green," "socially responsible," "fair trade" or other such goods and services. Consumers, on the other hand, are being encouraged to want them. While the ensuing relationships may be personable and the supply chain shorter and more innovative, the critical bonds and concerns still remain largely economic. Success is measured (and rationalized) in terms of profit generation, customer retention, and capital efficiency.[13]

DeLind suggests that if we are to truly build communities to support and expand local food systems that will allow local food to become a true alternative and even replacement for industrial food in its various guises (Roundup-resistant corn, processed foods, factory pork), then we must cultivate "the emotional, spiritual, and physical glue . . . not to a product but to layered sets of embodied relationships" and create deep connections to the people and places where local food is produced.[14] The difficulty of achieving this is deeply rooted in our commitment to individualism and an econometric view of relationships: "our mobility, our addiction to the virtual and to the individual, our immersion in the functional specialization of industrial society, and our dependence on market-encrusted relations all work against" developing communities of producers and consumers jointly committed to the welfare of specific local places and peoples.[15]

In short, building community is challenging work. It depends on a skill set many farmers may not possess (in particular skills to communicate, educate, and mobilize people to join a movement or market), and requires time that is often in short supply for farmers and other producers. It is not clear from my data whether stronger community-building efforts would strengthen and help the local food system grow, but it might be a short-term strategy that could pay dividends, as suggested by the pandemic experiences of farmers and chefs as described in the preceding section. However, if DeLind and others are correct, then the future of local food may depend on a cultural revolution to jettison the values and practices of the market and to embrace the values and practices that place community interest over self-interest, and make us committed defenders of the local.

Morality, Emotions, and Social Action

I began this study with a set of empirical questions: How does someone decide to get involved in a local food market? What sustains them through the difficult challenges of making a farm or other agricultural endeavor viable? How did the local food market in central New York develop? Sociologically, these questions also are questions about the forces that compel individuals to embark on some course of action and not others. Explaining action lies at the heart of sociology, and it is a task that has vexed many, because the motivations and causes of action are complicated, indirect, or hard to discern. As I sought answers to my research questions, my interviewees pointed me in the direction of morality and emotions, and they helped me see the interrelationships between their moral codes, the emotions triggered by producing local food, and the actions involved in their work. The stories they recounted, their answers to my interview questions, and the interactions I observed of them at various markets led me to several insights about morality, emotions, and action.

First, my interviewees see farming and local food production fundamentally as moral activities because they affect the health and well-being of consumers and communities, and because they reflect producers' understandings of the good self and the good life. Interviewees embraced an identity as a "good farmer" or "good chef," and such identities involved imperatives about how they should carry out their work and what goals they should pursue. The means and ends of local food were encapsulated in their commitments to care for the earth and its creatures; to ensure that their food was safe, healthy, and flavorful; and to promote community, solidarity, honesty, and/or justice. Following their moral code and realizing their goals about stewardship or sustainability required them to follow specific agricultural or culinary practices. For example, following organic methods for addressing pests and diseases allows a farmer to grow healthier crops and therefore realize the good farmer identity. In other words, local food producers' practices are intertwined with their sense of a moral self, and the more deeply one is committed to that self, the more likely it is that one's production and marketing practices will be congruent.[16]

Second, local food producers' moral codes appear to lock individuals into particular courses of action. Moral codes powerfully influence behavior because the individual, relational, and market costs of deviation may be too high to incur. Recall that local food markets target consumers who are willing to pay higher prices for produce and meat that they believe are tastier, healthier, and safer. A decision to abandon organic practices, for example, might alienate some consumers or even be seen as a violation of a trust relationship between farmer and CSA subscriber or regular farmers' market shopper. The sanctity of the trust relationship was apparent in my observations of farmers and shoppers at the various farmers' markets as discussed in chapter 4. Given the low profit rates of many farmers and the uncertainty of local food markets, deviating from their moral code may threaten their economic interests. However, as I discussed in earlier chapters, economic concerns were overshadowed by concerns about relationships, community, and living authentically. Many farmers and chefs are embedded in relationships of mutual support and aid. They turn to one another to solve problems, get advice, and/or share resources, which, in turn, help them hold fast to their preferred farming practices and realize their vision for local food. Recall chef Scott Ingalls's comment that he is "in the relationship business" more than the restaurant business. His commitment to locavore cooking is also a commitment to the ongoing relationships he has with a dozen or more farmers, foragers, cheesemakers, and wineries. Others' moral code stems from family traditions and both the real and remembered familial relationships. For example, Dan Nowak spoke about how he learned so much about farming from his father and how he aimed to follow in his footsteps, and Zack Jones of Black Creek Ranch talked about his goals of wanting to expand and improve the herd of cattle and land he inherited from his father and grandfather even as they lived next door. Thus, they adhere to a particular moral code as a means of fulfilling the legacy of their forebearers. More generally, moral codes come to be understood as binding and powerful to the degree that individuals are embedded in relationships in which following a shared code is critical to maintaining those relationships.

Third, moral codes are followed and constrain action because they are central to the identities of local food producers. Particular courses of action help individuals develop a moral self, and continued enactment of behaviors may verify both role-specific and a more global understanding of one's identity.[17] The good farmer or the good chef was not simply a role, but was central to local food producers' identities. Social psychologists suggest that "the individual is motivated to maintain and enhance it [the core self], to conceive of it as efficacious and consequential, and to experience it as meaningful and real."[18] We see this in how Melissa Harrison's and Liam Cook's identities as individuals who are committed to principles of justice led them to organize their CSAs so that people from lower incomes could have access to fresh produce, and in doing so reinforced their core identities.

Another insight from research about morality, action, and self is that following one's moral code heightens one's sense of efficacy in the world and authenticity, both of which are key motivations for action.[19] In their accounts about the ways in which they felt enchanted during agricultural work, farmers showed how those experiences offered feedback, really assurances, that they are called to the job and that they are their true self when farming. For many, their moral code stressed that to be a good person meant that they should be honest and transparent in their market relationships, and that they should be good stewards of the land. "Identity and the moral are deeply intertwined in the unfolding narrative of a person's life as a kind of quest to find a sense to that life."[20] The stories related by many of my interviewees dovetail with this claim. By enacting these values in their work of producing local food, farmers and others came to more fully see themselves as moral, and it reinforced their identities.

The critical role emotions play for cuing action and reaffirming identity is the final insight I have gained from the project. The activity of growing or producing food for the local market triggered strong emotions such as joy, pride, hope, and even defiance, and often generated a state of enchantment for individuals. The experience or situation of enchantment is the first of two important ways that emotions activate moral codes and action. Enchantment operates physically and cognitively. Emotions or affect must be interpreted, and those enchanting experiences on the farm or in the kitchen helped producers gain a sense of their authentic self or their true purpose. Social psychologist Peggy Thoits notes that "people are more likely to enact identities to which intense positive affect is attached.... Identity enactments in turn should influence feelings. Successful identity performances generate positive affect (e.g., self-esteem or pride in self); inadequate performances produce negative emotions (embarrassment or shame in self)."[21] Thoits suggests that action, identity, and emotions work in tandem to reinforce one another. For example, the fear of letting down one's customers may compel local food producers to follow their moral code about how to produce food, while the joy a farmer experiences when producing the best-tasting garlic or strawberries may confirm their belief that they are doing the right thing.

At the same time, emotions involve the body—the physical acts of farming and producing food (from pulling carrots from the ground, to mucking out stables, to cooking the perfect lamb chop and plating it) can provoke joy, pride, and excitement, which in turn help one develop and affirm one's moral habitus and moral self-hood. Sayer claims that emotions are "a kind of bodily commentary on how we, and our concerns are faring."[22] Emotions, then, not only serve as cues that producers use to appraise their choices, activities, and identities, but ultimately may lead to a high degree of alignment between code and agricultural conduct. Writing about religious practices (and farming may carry sacred overtones for some), Winchester notes how practices such as prayer or fasting help individuals come to see themselves as new types of moral beings and each time one engages in such practices, a "moral sense of one's place—[i.e.,] a degree of comfort with the possibilities and limits of living up to a moral identity" is reinforced.[23] Keith Stevens's comments about the joy he experiences watching things grow and how that experience keeps him farming illustrate the importance of the body-emotion-moral code connection. Similarly, I heard this when Dan Nowak described the ways in which he assesses the health of his soil and then carefully applies amendments in keeping with his stewardship orientation and identity.

Interaction, especially with customers, represents a second key moment in which the emotions of the encounter activate farmers' values and sense of their moral self. As discussed in the preceding chapter, farmers' encounters with shoppers at farmers' markets often generated a range of emotions—from pride and joy to discouragement and even anger (e.g., when shoppers complained about prices and called into question the value of the farmer's life work)—and both types of emotional encounters also produced emotional energies. These encounters and the buzz of emotional energies, especially when they feed into longer-lasting moods, served to confirm or reinforce farmers' commitment to local food, their choices of how to grow, as well as their self-understanding as the "good farmer."[24]

***

The endeavor to produce local food goes far beyond the work of growing vegetables, making cheese, or producing a first-class restaurant meal. It is entangled in a much wider set of social goals. It involves the effort to craft a sense of self and the good life. It is part of efforts to reduce the effects of climate change, promote biodiversity, and heal the earth. It is an attempt to create healthier, safer, and tastier food and change how Americans eat. It aims to build relationships among and between farmers, chefs, and consumers that rest on much more than monetary exchange. Writing about an upstate New York CSA, food scholar Caitlin Morgan argues that local food produces commensality: "The name invokes not only the practices of sitting down to a shared meal but also the feelings that arise from that practice.... The interdependency and reciprocity that develop. The community created by shared experience."[25] In this statement, she captures much of what I heard, observed, experienced, and learned during the years of studying local food. The intertwining of community and emotion, of ethics and action, of relationality and reciprocity—these are the promises of the local food movement, some realized and some still a hope to come.

ACKNOWLEDGMENTS

Books are collective endeavors, and while my name is on the front cover, a great many people helped me write and edit this volume. I am indebted to the farmers, chefs, cheesemakers, retailers, and all the others who spoke with me about their work and about local food in the region. They invited me into their homes, barns, and fields and patiently shared with me their knowledge of farming and food. While it is a truism to say that the book would not have been possible without them, it bears stating this explicitly. Colleagues at Hamilton and Colgate read early versions of chapters 1, 2, and 3. Dan Chambliss, Matt Grace, Chris Henke, Yagmur Karaya, Jaime Kucinskas, Alex Manning, and Mahala Stewart pushed me to develop the sociological argument, and the extent that I have succeeded rests on their assistance. In the early phase of the project, I worked with several Hamilton College faculty members on a grant proposal for a more expansive study. Alex Plakias, Peter Simons, Julie Starr, and Aaron Strong pushed me to clarify my ideas and to think more deeply about morality and food. Aaron suggested the title of the book during one of our meetings.

Several Hamilton College students served as research assistants during the first year of data collection: Nora McEntee, Julia McGuire, Amarilys Milian, and Kaitlyn Thayer. The Arthur C. Levitt Center at the college provided the funding for this group of students during the summer of 2018. The idea for the project itself emerged after I supervised Caty Taborda's 2011 senior fellowship at Hamilton about alternative food systems in the United States. I am not a rural sociologist, so I spent much of the year reading every book and article Caty did in order to more effectively supervise her project. I was intrigued by the literature and her interviews with farmers and activists. I began paying attention to what was going on at the local farmers' markets and started teaching a sociology of food course to deepen my knowledge and understanding of agriculture and food. Without the opportunity to supervise Caty, I most likely would never have decided to study local food.

Finally, I am thankful for the steadfast support of my family through yet another project that pulled me away or kept me preoccupied. I collected much of the data and wrote most of the book around the soccer training and rehab schedule of my youngest son, Mesafint. Our conversations on those regular car rides to Rochester where he trained, to Syracuse for twice-weekly rehab sessions, or across the Northeast for games and tournaments served as vivid reminders that there are more important things in this world than local food and one's research. I dedicate this book to him.

APPENDIX

Study Participants

CSAS

Cook, Liam	Harmony Farm
Harrison, Melissa	Hidden Hills Farm
Mahoney, Theresa	Three Willows Farm
Owens, Kate	Sleepy Hollow Farm
Rollins, Jamie	White Oak Farm
Stevens, Keith	Red Maple Farm
Weber, Paul	Stillwater Farm

MEAT PRODUCERS

Donovan, Laura and Nick	Quiet Springs Farm
Jones, Zack	Black Creek Ranch
Peters, Ed	Lucky Acres Farm
Robbins, Dave	Rocky Top Farm
Rose, Greg	Rolling Hills Farm
Stephenson, Lori	Foothills Farm
Wilson, Sarah and Tom	Twin Ponds Farm

SPECIALTY OR SMALL FAMILY FARMS

Anderson, David	Green Pastures Specialty Crops
Green, Julia	Green Family Farm
Kowalski, Jim and Yvette	Ridgeline Farm
Nielsen, Robert	Clear Brook Farm
Nowak, Dan	Valley View Farm
Tompkins, Mike and Riley	The Mushroomery
Wilson, Scott	Wilson Farm

APPENDIX

CHEESEMAKERS

Allen, Ken and Barbara	High Meadow Dairy
Bruckner, Jacob	Bruckner Dairy
Graham, Lisa	Woodside Creamery
Yoder, Lawrence	Sweet Clover Creamery

RESTAURANTS AND BREWERIES

Cook, Sam	The Leatherstocking Inn
Cooper, Larry	Green Gables Eatery
Davidson, Rick	Village Brewery
Duncan, Nick	Farmstead Brewery
Ellis, James	City Diner
Ingalls, Scott	Union Park Café
Russell, Thad	City Diner
Sloan, Nancy	Lakeshore Bistro
White, Brett	The Foodshed

RETAIL OR AGRICULTURAL SUPPORT ORGANIZATIONS

Clark, Seth	Green Garden Natural Food Store
Constantino, Nick	Agricultural nonprofit
Davis, Steve	Harvest Moon Health Foods
Ellis, Larry	Central New York Farm Co-op
Fuller, Melissa	Farmers' market manager
Hart, Beth and Taylor	The Garden Store and Food Processing Incubator
Hughes, Andrea	Farmers' market manager
Michelson, Britt	Agricultural nonprofit
Noyes, Ken	Agricultural nonprofit
Rogers, Blaine	The Locavore
Williams, Karen	Farmers' market manager
Warren, Mark	Agricultural nonprofit

NOTES

CHAPTER 1. WHAT IS LOCAL FOOD AND WHY IS IT IMPORTANT?

1. Griffin and Frongillo (2003) note that weather, rising costs for farm inputs such as fuel, fertilizers, or seeds, and creating a stable market or base of customers are major challenges for farmers who produce for a local market.
2. Farrell, 2015: 9–10.
3. For example, MacKendrick, 2018; and DeVault, 1991.
4. See Ross, 2006; Macias, 2008; Schrank, 2014; and Trivette, 2017.
5. Dowler et al., 2010: 212 (italics original). See also Stock, 2021; Shisler and Sbicca, 2019; Cox et al., 2016.
6. Grauel (2016: 854) notes,
   > First, national health policies aiming at governing individual food habits and media discourses around nutrition, food risks, and environmental challenges confront large parts of the population of western societies with moral claims on how to consume food. Second, food shopping and eating have been shown to relate to multiple moral issues within everyday life, for example caring for household members, demarcating the realm of "authentic" family life from the market, the construction of family identity as well as being thrifty and eating healthily. (Parenthetical in-text citations omitted)
7. Sage, 2003.
8. Janssen, 2017.
9. Low et al., 2015.
10. Tropp, 2014. On CSAs, see Woods, Ernst, and Tropp, 2017.
11. The designation "central New York" varies and for this study includes eight counties that generally run along the I-90 corridor between Syracuse in the west and Amsterdam in the east: Madison, Chenango, Oneida, Otsego, Herkimer, Fulton, Montgomery, and Schoharie.
12. I identified these figures by searching through the county-level data of the 2017 USDA Agricultural Census for the counties in the research study, www.nass.usda.gov, accessed June 21, 2021.
13. For county-level statistics, see Cornell Program on Applied Demographics, https://pad.human.cornell.edu, accessed June 21, 2021.
14. On the artisanal revival, see Ocejo, 2018; Heying, 2010; and Bowen and De Master, 2014. On artisanal or craft producers making intentional efforts to

challenge the hegemony of corporate commodity food production, see Paxson, 2012; Carroll and Swaminathan, 2000; and Rao, 2009.
15 See Belasco, 2007 [1989].
16 Lapping, 2004. Others have also noted the role of food safety in the development of local food systems; see, for example, Qazi and Selfa, 2005; DeLind, 2006; and Schrank, 2014.
17 Mikulak, 2013: 44. See also Obach, 2015; and Haedicke, 2016.
18 The facile equation of local with ecologically sound or morally superior is problematic, as numerous scholars have pointed out. There are no guarantees that local farmers do not use pesticides or genetically modified crops, or more generally rely on sustainable agricultural practices. See Hinrichs, 2003; Dupuis and Goodman, 2005; Schnell, 2013; and Trivette, 2015.
19 Allen and Hinrichs, 2007.
20 For an overview, see Goldstein, 2013.
21 DeLind, 2006.
22 Thompson and Press, 2014.
23 Ostrom, 2006.
24 Note that these are ideals and not necessarily embodied or held by all participants in local food systems. This list is derived from my reading of the scholarly and popular literature about local food. See Janssen, 2017; Mikulak, 2013; Robinson and Farmer, 2017; Ostrom, 2006; Allen, 2004; and Kloppenburg, Hendrickson, and Stevenson, 2000.
25 Ferguson, 1998.
26 Johnston and Baumann, 2007: 171. See also Johnston and Baumann, 2009, 2015 [2010].
27 Mayer, 2014: 69.
28 Smith, 2005: 8.
29 Polletta, 2006: 13 (italics added).
30 Polletta (2006: 14) makes this point in more detail in her "sociology of storytelling."
31 Farrell, 2015: 15. See also Mayer, 2014: 53–64.
32 Polletta, 2006: 12. See also Mayer, 2014: 72–73, 138–39; and Fine and Sandstrom, 1993.
33 For a summary of alternative food writing, see Johnston and Baumann, 2009. See also Pollan, 2010; Mikulak, 2013; Haedicke, 2016: 25–41; and Kennedy, Johnston, and Parkins, 2017.
34 Johnston and Baumann, 2009; Mikulak, 2013.
35 Mikulak, 2013: 89.
36 Pollan, 2006a.
37 Pollan, 2006b: 240–41.
38 Pollan, 2008: 158.
39 My analysis of local food journalism examines articles found in *Saveur, Bon Appetit, Food & Wine*, and *Gourmet*, essays collected in the *Best Food Writing* (2006–2018),

and key popular monographs that champion local or alternative agriculture, including Nabhan, 2002; Kingsolver, 2007; Pollan, 2006b, 2008; and Barber, 2014. I had limited access to food magazines but have the most complete access to *Bon Appetit* (2007–2020) and *Saveur* (2009–2019). I had digital access to the final two years of *Gourmet* (2007–2009) and 2015–2020 for *Food & Wine*. This type of food journalism largely caters to an upper-middle- and upper-class, college-educated audience who are more likely to have the level of income necessary to purchase the often more expensive local foods. The three magazines still in print have a print audience that range from 444,000 to 8 million; a digital readership that ranges from 2.3 to 12.3 million, and a similar number of social media followers. I used the following terms to search for articles about local food: "local food," "locavore," "farm to table," "farm to fork," "farm to institution," "community supported agriculture," "farmers' market," and "farmstead." The search yielded 35 articles in *Bon Appetit*, 38 in *Saveur*, 15 in *Gourmet*, 18 in *Food & Wine*, and 40 in the various volumes of *Best Food Writing*. The database of 146 articles is as complete as I could develop, but I acknowledge that it is incomplete and may underestimate the number of local food stories. I also did not include short lists of local restaurants or food types, or articles that mentioned "local food" only in passing.

40 Several authors structure popular books about local food around pioneer stories as well. See Gayeton, 2014; Cobb, 2011; and Ryder and Topalian, 2010.
41 Nabhan, 2002: 26–27.
42 Nabhan, 2002: 304.
43 McKibben, 2006; this is an excerpt from McKibben, 2007.
44 Anderson, 2008.
45 On the plot of comedy, see White, 1973: 8–10. See also Frye, 1957; and Mayer, 2014: 61.
46 Pollan, 2006b, 2008.
47 Kessler, 2013.
48 Kessler, 2013: 156, 158.
49 Black, 2019.
50 Mayer, 2014: 59–61.
51 On the ways in which stories gain power by introducing novelty or variations of plot or characters, see Cawelti, 1976: 10–12.
52 Cunningham, 2012: 40.
53 See Sayer, 2011: 36–39; Ignatow, 2009; and Bandelj, 2009.
54 Farrell notes that "humans are believers embedded in stories big and small that separate sacred from profane and tell us who we are, why we are, what we are and why it all matters. . . . Stories direct our lives and make what we do significant" (2015: 11).
55 See Mathews, 1992; and Strauss, 1992.
56 Farrell, 2015: 12.
57 Pole and Gray, 2012; DeLind, 2002; Hinrichs, 2000.

58 Guthman, 2008a; Alkon, 2012; Lynch and Giles, 2013.
59 Papaoikonomou and Ginieis, 2016; Gray, 2014; Ross, 2006.
60 DeLind, 2011; Guthman, 2008b; Hinrichs, 2003; Allen et al., 2003.
61 Contemporary pastoralism combines a commitment to the ecological value of sustainability and stewardship with the older Jeffersonian virtues of autonomy, hard work, and community. See Press and Arnould, 2011.
62 In particular, values play a prominent role in the work of Max Weber, Emile Durkheim, and Talcott Parsons.
63 Smith, 2009: 51. He is not the only sociologist who shares this assumption and whose empirical works (or the works they cite) support the claim. See also Farrell, 2015; Barnard, 2016; Hitlin and Vaisey, 2013; Tavory, 2011; Sayer, 2005a; Hardy and Carlo, 2005; Hoey, 2005; and Monroe, 2001.
64 Sayer, 2011: 1.
65 Sayer, 2005a: 952.
66 Sayer, 2005b: 8.
67 Farrell, 2015: 10. See also Wuthnow, 1987 for a wide-ranging discussion of the relationship between ideology, ritual on the one hand and moral codes and moral orders on the other.
68 Geertz, 1973: 127.
69 Fourcade and Healy, 2007. See also Wuthnow, 1996; and Zelizer, 1979.
70 Fine, 1998: 7.
71 Fine, 1998: 36–37.
72 Farrell, 2015: 12.
73 Weiler, Otero, and Wittman, 2016. See also Dowler et al., 2010; and Kloppenburg, Hendrickson, and Stevenson, 1996.
74 See Swidler, 2001, 2008, 1986.
75 The tool kit account of action is not a satisfying explanation in part because it doesn't provide a way to understand how individuals use the contents of their tool kits to guide their action, and in part because values seem to have little role in social life except to help us justify our actions after the fact. Morality seems arbitrary at best, as humans will switch values as opportunities arise, or moral values themselves are secondary to finding an action that will best fit a given situation or context. Barnard (2016: 1020) argues that the tool kit approach makes morality a utilitarian tool of impression management and unmoors morality from any kind of center for the individual or group. Vaisey (2009: 1680–81) argues that Swidler's "tool kit" explanation for action is flawed because it rests on an assumption that action and moral motivations must consistently match, and they often do not (i.e., we hold one set of values that should make us act one way but we act in ways that violate those allegedly motivating values).
76 Fine and Sandstrom, 1993.
77 Sayer, 2005b: 48; Sayer, 2011: 27. See also Ignatow, 2009; Lively and Powell, 2006; Hardy and Carlo, 2005; and Thoits, 1989.

78 Bourdieu, 1993: 5–6.
79 Sayer, 2005b: 42–50. The inclusion of morality or values into the habitus is an important corrective to Bourdieu's concept because he tended to downplay the role of morality and talked about it only in terms of how actors craft evaluative standards to draw boundaries between groups and as a means to exercise and maintain power relations. See also Ignatow, 2009.
80 Swidler, 2001: 169.
81 See, for example, Winchester and Green, 2019; Fine, 2009 [1996]; and Kunda, 2006.
82 See Boltanski and Thevenot, 2006; Pecoraro and Uusitalo, 2014; and Stamer, 2018.
83 Biggart and Beamish, 2003, as cited in Ponte, 2016: 13.
84 Sayer, 2005b: 50–51.
85 Stock, 2007: 88. See also Carolan, 2020; Sutherland and Darnhofer, 2012; Burton, 2004; and Kaltoff, 1999.
86 Hoey, 2005: 592.
87 Hoey, 2005: 592.
88 See Hardy and Hardy, 2005; Monroe, 2001; Barnard, 2016.
89 Tavory, 2011.
90 Tavory, 2011: 281.
91 Turner and Stets (2006: 29) summarize the symbolic interactionist explanation of the ties between action and emotions:

> The basic generalizations of all symbolic interactionists' theories are that individuals seek to confirm their more global self-conceptions as well as their more context dependent identities in all episodes of interaction. When self is verified by others responding to self in a manner that is consistent with self's own view, the person experiences positive emotions, such as pride and satisfaction. When self is not conformed, however, the incongruity between self-directed behavior and the responses of others generates negative emotions such as distress, anxiety, anger, shame, and guilt.

See also Thoits, 1989; Scheff, 1988; and Lively and Powell, 2006.
92 Sayer, 2005b: 948.
93 Bandelj, 2009: 352.
94 Collins, 2004: 109 (see his discussion of emotional energy and moods on pp. 105–6). See also Jasper, 2011: 291. He argues that the combinations of positive and negative emotions may form "moral batteries" in which the stored energy "motivates action or demands attention" when activated during specific situations.
95 On the different types of emotions, see Jasper, 2011.
96 Ignatow, 2008: 106.
97 I was unable to find any producers who are not white, which, given the demographics of the region, is not surprising. Although there is a small population of refugees from southeast Asia, Africa, and Latin America, and a small native black

population, their agricultural endeavors were confined to producing for their own consumption in community gardens or small leased farms.

98 Hughes, 1994; Ashforth and Kreiner, 1999; Simpson et al., 2012.

CHAPTER 2. THE MORAL FOUNDATIONS OF LOCAL FOOD PRODUCTION

1 Greenhorns are "first generation farmers with no family connection to agriculture for at least two generations." Bruce, 2019: 33.
2 See Allen and Bernhardt, 1995; Beus and Dunlap, 1994; and Parks and Brekken, 2019.
3 Thompson, 2010: 207.
4 Holthaus, 2006: 277–28.
5 Worster, 1984: 39.
6 Bruce, 2019; Beingessner and Fletcher, 2020; Albrecht and Smithers, 2018; Griffin and Frongillo, 2003; Wells, Gradwell, and Yoder, 2002.
7 Thompson, 2010: 39. On the goal or ideal of building community within the local food movement, see Schnell, 2013; Albrecht and Smithers, 2018; Allen and Hinrichs, 2007; and Wells, Gradwell, and Yoder, 2002. On the lack of interest or limits of building community, see Pole and Gray, 2012; and Papaoikonomou and Ginieis, 2016.
8 Stock, 2007: 96.
9 Weber, Heinze, and DeSoucey, 2008: 543. See also Hardy and Carlo, 2005.
10 Michaelson, 2009: 30.
11 Barnard, 2016: 1021. See also Winchester, 2008.
12 Thompson and Coskuner-Balli, 2007b, 2007a.
13 On the sociology of the role of emotions in guiding identity and action and serving as a feedback mechanism, see Mills and Kleinman, 1988; Jasper, 1988, 2011; Turner and Stets, 2006; and Collins, 2004.
14 The connections between embodied action and the moral self are well articulated by Winchester, 2016, 2008.
15 On food miles, see Trivette, 2015.
16 Bruce (2019: 33) also found that greenhorns' middle-class and family resources played a key role in facilitating their entry into local food production.
17 Stock, 2007: 96.
18 Bruce, 2019: 34.
19 Ellis, 2013: 436.
20 The farmers in my study resemble the returning farmers that Bruce (2019) interviewed. In her research, she found that those with a farming background who returned later in life did so because they may have seen farming as a more fulfilling job than their non-farm work; because they saw a return as a way to enact deeply held social and environmental concerns of the local food movement; and/or because it was a means to address health and family commitments.

21 Weber, Heinze, and DeSoucey write about the motives that drive those in the grass-fed beef market: "Motivational models of entrepreneurship often focus on instrumental motivations that drive entrepreneurs, such as expectations about financial gains. We found that the financial motivation certainly mattered, because producers had to make a living from farming. Nevertheless, the decision to enter and persist in this particular market benefited from the availability of a broader vocabulary of motives provided by the movement's cultural codes [i.e., authenticity and honesty, sustainability, and conservation]" (2008: 542–43).
22 "In zone tillage, a narrow band of soil is tilled shallowly where planting will take place, and soil between crop rows is undisturbed. For example, a planting row may be tilled a few inches wide and a few inches deep in soils without a compaction layer. Undisturbed soil between rows may contain cover crop or green manure crop residue that protects it from erosion and moisture loss. Zone tillage combines some of the benefits of no-till production with the soil-warming benefits of tillage." Goranson, Johnson, and English, n.d.
23 The concept of "emotional insights" is from Mills and Kleinman, 1988: 1020.
24 Turner and Stets, 2006: 32.
25 This discussion of the connections between emotions, self, and action draws on the insights from Jasper, 2011; and Winchester and Green, 2019.
26 Fine, 2009 [1996].
27 Lane, 2014: 71; see also Leschziner, 2010.
28 Fairfax et al., 2012: 129. See also Goldstein, 2013; Trubek, 2008 (esp. chaps. 4 and 5); and Belasco, 2007 [1989].
29 Inwood et al., 2009.
30 Nelson, Beckie, and Krogman, 2017. See also VanWinkle, 2017.
31 See Nelson, Beckie, and Krogman, 2017; Van Winkle, 2017; and Inwood et al., 2009, as well as Thomas McNamee's biography of pioneering locavore chef Alice Waters (McNamee, 2007) and Dan Barber's (2014) call to reimagine local cuisine by building more equitable and useful relationships between producers and chefs.
32 According to the chef, the region has been given this moniker because the population and the number of restaurants are very low between Albany and Syracuse.
33 On the turn to older culinary arts in locavore kitchens, see Nelson, Beckie, and Krogman, 2017: 511–12; and Van Winkle, 2017.
34 See Sayer, 2005b: 25.

CHAPTER 3. BUILDING THE LOCAL FOODSHED

1 Bell, 2004.
2 Some scholars argue that all markets are inherently moral, insofar as exchange rests on trust, but not all markets are constructed intentionally to be understood publicly as moral. More generally, moral markets are those that rely on both social and economic values to coordinate exchange. See McInerney, 2014; Fourcade and Healy, 2007; and Zelizer, 1979.

3 On the economy of regard, see Offer, 1997.
4 Hinrichs, 2000.
5 For a popular critique of conventional agriculture's production of cheap and plentiful food, see Pollan, 2008, 2006b.
6 On the imperatives of creating a market, see Weber, Heinze, and DeSoucey, 2008; and Fligstein and Dauter, 2007.
7 Soil fertility was identified by a group of Canadian locavore farmers as critical to their work. See Beingessner and Fletcher, 2020: 135.
8 On holistic management, see "Why Holistic Management," Holistic Management International, https://holisticmanagement.org, accessed May 31, 2021. On regenerative agriculture, see "What Is Regenerative Agriculture?," unpublished paper by Regenerative Agriculture Initiative, California State University, Chico, and Carbon Underground, https://regenerationinternational.org, accessed May 31, 2021. In this document, regenerative agriculture is defined in the following way:
> Regenerative Agriculture is a holistic land management practice that leverages the power of photosynthesis in plants to close the carbon cycle, and build soil health, crop resilience and nutrient density. Regenerative agriculture improves soil health, primarily through the practices that increase soil organic matter. This not only aids in increasing soil biota diversity and health, but increases biodiversity both above and below the soil surface, while increasing both water holding capacity and sequestering carbon at greater depths, thus drawing down climate-damaging levels of atmospheric CO_2, and improving soil structure to reverse civilization-threatening human-caused soil loss. . . . Well-managed grazing practices stimulate improved plant growth, increased soil carbon deposits, and overall pasture and grazing land productivity while greatly increasing soil fertility, insect and plant biodiversity, and soil carbon sequestration. These practices not only improve ecological health, but also the health of the animal and human consumer through improved micro-nutrients availability and better dietary omega balances. Feed lots and confined animal feeding systems contribute dramatically to (i) unhealthy monoculture production systems, (ii) low nutrient density forage, (iii) increased water pollution, (iv) antibiotic usage and resistance, and (v) CO_2 and methane emissions, all of which together yield broken and ecosystem-degrading food-production systems.

9 See Griffin and Frongillo, 2003; Beingessner and Fletcher, 2020; Robinson and Farmer, 2017; Janssen, 2017; Albrecht and Smithers, 2018; Schrank, 2014; and Trivette, 2016.
10 Allen et al., 2003: 64. At the same time, scholars have offered telling critiques about the limits of local or alternative agriculture to operate as a moral market. Some pointedly show how it fails to promote community and others that price and instrumentalism guide marketplace behavior. See Papaoikonomou and Ginieis, 2016; Gray, 2014; Ross, 2006; and Hinrichs, 2000. However, I am

concerned more here with how the market is organized to promote a morality of food rather than how well it achieves this goal.
11 See Parkins and Craig, 2009; Sage, 2003; and Lee, 2000.
12 Kloppenburg, Hendrickson, and Stevenson, 1996.
13 Rules about who can and cannot sell at farmers' markets in order to minimize competition and maximize profit are not unique to central New York. See Mars and Schau, 2017.
14 On the nature and practices of cooperative networks among alternative farmers who sell at farmers' markets, see Chiffoleau, 2009.
15 Griffin and Frongillo, 2003: 197. See also Stock, 2007; Thompson and Coskuner-Balli, 2007a; and Parks and Brekken, 2019.
16 Durrenberger, 2002. On CSA and community building, see Janssen, 2010; Macias, 2008; and Wells, Gradwell, and Yoder, 2002.
17 For a rich discussion of the meanings attached to "community," see Keller, 2003.
18 Pole and Gray, 2012; Papaoikonomou and Ginieis, 2016.
19 In his study of fair trade, Keith Brown also discusses the challenges of moral markets: "Both the promoters and the conscientious consumers with whom I spoke, all of whom were recruited while shopping at fair-trade retail stores, worked hard to avoid talking directly about moral issues. They used savvy justification strategies to redirect conversations away from ethical issues and towards subjects like price, utility, quality, and taste" (Brown, 2013: 93). He concludes the book by noting how fair-trade promoters avoid drawing distinctions between fair trade and conventionally produced products because they do not wish to tell others how they ought to consume or judge them for their consumption practices, and prefer to not be viewed as "too preachy" by their potential customers (140).
20 See data for 2019 collected by the USDA, www.ers.usda.gov, accessed June 11, 2022.
21 "FoodAPS National Household Food Acquisition and Purchase Survey," USDA, www.ers.usda.gov, accessed June 11, 2021.
22 Even when conventional grocery stores attempt to incorporate local foods into their regular product lines, the process and outcome often shortchange local producers and distributors/brokers as stores' goals of centralization, efficiency, and cost savings appear to take the local out of local. One recent study of Walmart's effort to add local foods to its grocery offerings summarized the less than ideal outcomes:
> Its lean retailing model for implementing local produce sourcing in the US Wal-Mart's highly centralized structure and distribution networks (including use of "local" category managers) made it difficult for smaller-scale producers to access its local produce market. Direct-store-deliveries and large-scale growers acting as intermediaries did enhance integration of smaller-scale growers into Wal-Mart's locally grown program. However,

DSD relationships sat uneasily with Wal-Mart's centralized management and infrastructure, and intermediaries incurred additional costs and risks in working with small-scale growers, while also facing the potential of being bypassed by Wal-Mart. Further, Wal-Mart's default to a national, centralized pricing structure for local produce failed to account for unique growing conditions and constraints in different geographical regions, which can mean higher costs and shorter growing periods for some producers than in other areas, and therefore the need for higher prices. Finally, Wal-Mart's treatment of local produce as simply another "category" and its attempts to standardize local products with a generic company-wide label further disembedded local produce from its social, environmental and farm contexts, in a move sometimes resisted and certainly questioned by the very local producers it sought to enroll. (Bloom and Hinrichs, 2017: 181)

23 Low et al., 2015.

CHAPTER 4. MORALITY, EMOTIONS, AND THE FUTURE OF LOCAL FOOD

1. Jordan, 2015: 117.
2. Philip Ackerman-Leist argues that "there isn't sufficient local infrastructure in place for processing, storing, distributing, and retailing agricultural goods" across the United States. This is critical because, he notes, "distribution drives the food system," and without a robust distribution system, farmers simply will not be able to get their products to market (2013: 14, 40).
3. A food hub, according to the USDA, "is a business or organization that actively manages the aggregation, distribution, and marketing of source-identified food products primarily from local and regional producers to strengthen their ability to satisfy wholesale, retail, and institutional demand." "Regional Food Hub Resource Guide," 2012, USDA Agricultural Marketing Service, 4, www.ams.usda.gov, accessed July 21, 2021.
4. The vegetable processing plant is organized as a co-op of midsize farmers (with farms of 100–200 acres) who grow peas, tomatoes, and beans, which are processed, packed, and then shipped out of state for sale at Walmart stores or to wholesalers in New York City, who in turn ship it all over the Eastern Seaboard. While the farmers are well served, the produce does not stay local.
5. Alkon and Guthman, 2017: 6.
6. Strasburg, 2020.
7. Westervelt, 2020a, 2020b. See also the following issues of *Gastronomica* for special sections about the food industry and COVID-19: vol. 20, nos. 3 & 4 (2020) and vol. 21, no. 1 (2021).
8. Belarmino et al., 2020; Gody, McGarry, and Tritten, 2020; Dale and Sharma, 2021.
9. Hinrichs and Barham, 2007.
10. Stevenson et al., 2007: 47. See also Janssen, 2010.

11 Ackerman-Leist, 2103: 51.
12 On local food institutions that fail to develop community but encourage only individual relationships between producer and consumer, see Papaoikonomou and Ginieis, 2016; Pole and Gray, 2012; Beingessner and Fletcher, 2020; Griffin and Frongillo, 2003; and Ross, 2006.
13 DeLind's critique follows others' arguments that local foods are championed as part of a more general critique of neoliberalism. See Guthman, 2008b: 1172.
14 DeLind, 2006: 126. See also DeLind, 2002.
15 DeLind, 2006: 129.
16 The literature on the good farmer supports this claim, as does some work on emotions and the self. In particular see Turner and Stets, 2006: 30–32; Frijda, 2004; and Schwalbe, 1991.
17 See Turner and Stets, 2006; Winchester, 2008; and Winchester and Green, 2019.
18 Gecas, 1991: 174. See also Monroe, 2001; Hardy and Carlo, 2005; and Stets and Carter, 2011, 2012.
19 Gecas, 1991: 174–79.
20 Hoey, 2005: 592.
21 Thoits, 1989: 332; see also Stets and Carter, 2012, 2011.
22 Sayer, 2011: 39.
23 Winchester, 2008. Quote is from Barnard, 2016: 1108–9.
24 This idea about how interactions create emotional energies that affirm moral commitments and identities draws on Collins's work about interaction ritual chains. However, few of the interactions that my interviewees described and that I witnessed meet the specific criteria of his theory (i.e., group assembly, barriers to outsiders). See Collins, 2004, esp. chaps. 3 and 4.
25 Morgan, 2020: 46.

REFERENCES

Ackerman-Leist, Philip. 2013. *Rebuilding the Food Shed: How to Create Local, Sustainable, and Secure Food Systems.* White River Junction, VT: Chelsea Green.

Albrecht, Cayla, and John Smithers. 2018. "Reconnecting through Local Food Initiatives? Purpose, Practice and Conceptions of Value." *Agriculture and Human Values* 35: 67–81.

Alkon, Allison Hope. 2012. *Black, White, and Green: Farmers Markets, Race, and the Green Economy.* Athens: University of Georgia Press.

Alkon, Allison Hope, and Julie Guthman. 2017. *Food Activism: Opposition, Cooperation, and Collective Action.* Berkeley: University of California Press.

Allen, John C., and Kevin Bernhardt. 1995. "Farming Practices and Adherence to an Alternative-Conventional Agricultural Paradigm." *Rural Sociology* 60 (2): 297–309.

Allen, Patricia. 2004. *Together at the Table: Sustainability and Sustenance in the American Agrifood System.* University Park: Pennsylvania State University Press.

Allen, Patricia, Margaret FitzSimmons, Michael Goodman, and Keith Warner. 2003. "Shifting Plates in the Agrifood Landscape: The Tectonics of Alternative Agrifood Initiatives in California." *Journal of Rural Studies* 19 (1): 61–75.

Allen, Patricia, and Claire Hinrichs. 2007. "Buying into 'Buy Local': Engagement of United States Local Food Initiatives." In *Alternative Food Geographies*, edited by D. Maye, L. Holloway, and M. Kneafsey, 255–71. New York: Elsevier.

Anderson, Mark C. 2008. "Miles to Go before I Eat." In *Best Food Writing, 2008*, edited by Holly Hughes, 36–45. Philadelphia: Da Capo.

Ashforth, Blake E., and Glen E. Kreiner. 1999. "'How Can You Do It?': Dirty Work and the Challenge of Constructing a Positive Identity." *Academy of Management Review* 24 (3): 413–34.

Bandelj, Nina. 2009. "Emotions in Economic Action and Interaction." *Theory and Society* 38 (4): 347–66.

Barber, Dan. 2014. *The Third Plate: Field Notes on the Future of Food.* New York: Penguin.

Barnard, Alex V. 2016. "Making the City 'Second Nature': Freegan 'Dumpster Divers' and the Materiality of Morality." *American Journal of Sociology* 121 (4): 1017–50.

Beingessner, Naomi, and Amber J. Fletcher. 2020. "Going Local: Farmers' Perspectives on Local Food Systems in Rural Canada." *Agriculture and Human Values* 37: 129–45.

Belarmino, Emily H., Farryl Bertmann, Thomas Wentworth, Erin Biehl, Roni Neff, and Meredith T. Niles. 2020. "The Impact of COVID-19 on the Local Food System:

Early Findings from Vermont." *Agriculture and Life Sciences Faculty Publications* 23: 1–3. https://scholarworks.uvm.edu.

Belasco, Warren J. 2007 [1989]. *Appetite for Change: How the Counterculture Took on the Food Industry*. Ithaca: Cornell University Press.

Bell, Michael Mayerfield. 2004. *Farming for Us All: Practical Agriculture and the Cultivation of Sustainability*. University Park: Pennsylvania State University Press.

Beus, Curtis E., and Riley E. Dunlap. 1994. "Agricultural Paradigms and the Practice of Agriculture." *Rural Sociology* 69 (4): 620–35.

Biggart, Nicole, and Thomas D. Beamish. 2003. "The Economic Sociology of Conventions: Habit, Custom, Practice, and Routine in Market Order." *Annual Review of Sociology* 29: 443–64.

Black, Jane. 2019. "Spike Gjerde Champions Local Food Economics: 8 Mid-Atlantic Makers to Know." *Food & Wine*, February 19, 2019.

Bloom, J. Dara, and C. Clare Hinrichs. 2017. "The Long Reach of Lean Retailing: Firm Embeddedness and Wal-Mart's Implementation of Local Produce Sourcing in the US." *Environment and Planning A* 49 (1): 168–85.

Boltanski, Luc, and Laurent Thevenot. 2006. *On Justification: Economies of Worth*. Princeton: Princeton University Press.

Bourdieu, Pierre. 1993. *The Field of Cultural Production*. New York: Columbia University Press.

Bowen, Sarah, and Kathryn De Master. 2014. "Wisconsin's Happy Cows? Articulating Heritage and Territory as New Dimensions of Locality." *Agriculture and Human Values* 31 (4): 549–62.

Brown, Keith R. 2013. *Buying into Fair Trade: Culture, Morality, and Consumption*. New York: New York University Press.

Bruce, Analena B. 2019. "Farm Entry and Persistence: Three Pathways into Alternative Agriculture in Southern Ohio." *Journal of Rural Studies* 69: 30–40.

Burton, Rob J. F. 2004. "Seeing through the 'Good Farmer's' Eyes: Towards Developing an Understanding of the Social Symbolic Value of 'Productivist' Behavior." *Sociologia Ruralis* 44 (2): 195–215.

Carolan, Michael. 2020. "Ethical Eating as Experienced by Consumers and Producers: When Good Food Meets Good Farmers." *Journal of Consumer Culture* 22 (1): 103–23.

Carroll, Glenn R., and Anand Swaminathan. 2000. "Why the Microbrewery Movement? Organizational Dynamics of Resource Partitioning in the US Brewing Industry." *American Journal of Sociology* 106 (3): 715–62.

Cawelti, John G. 1976. *Adventure, Mystery, and Romance*. Chicago: University of Chicago Press.

Chiffoleau, Yuna. 2009. "From Politics to Co-operation: The Dynamics of Embeddedness in Alternative Food Supply Chains." *Sociologia Ruralis* 49 (3): 218–35.

Cobb, Tanya Denckla. 2011. *Reclaiming Our Food: How the Grassroots Food Movement Is Changing the Way We Eat*. North Adams, MA: Storey Publishing.

Collins, Randall. 2004. *Interaction Ritual Chains*. Princeton: Princeton University Press.
Conroy, Thomas M., ed. 2014. *Food and Everyday Life*. Washington, DC: Lexington Books.
Counihan, Carole, ed. 2002. *Food in the USA: A Reader*. New York: Routledge.
Cox, Rosie, Moya Kneafsey, Lewis Holloway, Elizabeth Dowler, and Laura Venn. 2016. "Greater Than the Sum of the Parts? Unpacking Ethics of Care within a Community Supported Agriculture Scheme." In *Food Transgressions: Making Sense of Contemporary Food Politics*, edited by Michael K. Goodman and Colin Sage, 61–81. New York: Routledge.
Cunningham, Brent. 2012. "Pastoral Romance." In *The Best Food Writing, 2012*, edited by Holly Hughes, 36–47. Philadelphia: Da Capo.
Dale, Bryan, and Jayeeta Sharma. 2021. "Feeding the City, Pandemic and Beyond: A Research Brief." *Gastronomica* 21 (1): 86–91.
D'Andrade, Roy, and Claudia Strauss, eds. 1992. *Human Motives and Cultural Models*. New York: Cambridge University Press.
DeLind, Laura B. 2002. "Considerably More Than Vegetables, a Lot Less Than Community: The Dilemma of Community Supported Agriculture." In *Fighting for the Farm: Rural America Transformed*, edited by Jane Adams, 192–206. Philadelphia: University of Pennsylvania Press.
———. 2006. "Of Bodies, Place, and Culture: Resituating Local Food." *Journal of Agricultural and Environmental Ethics* 19: 121–46.
———. 2011. "Are Local Food and the Local Food Movement Taking Us Where We Want to Go? Or Are We Hitching Our Wagon to the Wrong Stars? *Agriculture and Human Values* 28: 273–83.
DeVault, Marjorie. 1991. *Feeding the Family: The Social Organization of Caring as Gendered Work*. Chicago: University of Chicago Press.
Dowler, Elizabeth, Moya Kneafsey, Rosie Cox, and Lewis Holloway. 2010. "'Doing Food Differently': Reconnecting Biological and Social Relationships through Care for Food." *Sociological Review* 57 (2, supplement): 200–220.
Dupuis, E. Melanie, and David Goodman. 2005. "Should We Go 'Home' to Eat? Toward a Reflexive Politics of Localism." *Journal of Rural Studies* 21: 359–71.
Durrenberger, Paul E. 2002. "Community Supported Agriculture in Central Pennsylvania." *Culture & Agriculture* 24 (2): 42–51.
Ellis, Colter. 2013. "The Symbiotic Ideology: Stewardship, Husbandry, and Dominion in Beef Production." *Rural Sociology* 78 (4): 429–49.
Fairfax, Sally K., Louise Nelson Dyble, Grieg Tor Guthey, Lauren Gwin, Monica Moore, and Jennifer Sokolove. 2012. *California Cuisine and Just Food*. Cambridge: MIT Press.
Farrar, James, ed. 2010. *Globalization, Food, and Social Identities in the Pacific Region*. Tokyo: Sophia University Institute of Comparative Culture.
Farrell, Justin. 2015. *The Battle for Yellowstone: Morality and the Sacred Roots of Environmental Conflict*. Princeton: Princeton University Press.

Ferguson, Priscilla Parkhurst. 1998. "A Cultural Field in the Making: Gastronomy in 19th-Century France." *American Journal of Sociology* 104 (3): 597–641.

Fine, Gary Alan. 1998. *Morel Tales: The Culture of Mushrooming*. Boston: Harvard University Press.

———. 2009 [1996]. *Kitchens: The Culture of Restaurant Work*. Chicago: University of Chicago Press.

Fine, Gary Alan, and Kent Sandstrom. 1993. "Ideology in Action: A Pragmatic Approach to a Contested Concept." *Sociological Theory* 11 (1): 21–38.

Fligstein, Neil, and Luke Dauter. 2007. "The Sociology of Markets." *Annual Review of Sociology* 33: 105–28.

Fourcade, Marion, and Kieran Healy. 2007. "Moral Views of Market Society." *Annual Review of Sociology* 33: 285–311.

Frank, Robert H. 1988. *Passions within Reason: The Strategic Role of the Emotions*. New York: Norton.

Frank, Sally K., Louise Nelson Dyble, Greig Tor Guthey, Lauren Gwin, Monica Moore, Jennifer Sokolove, and Marion Nestle. 2012. *California Cuisine and Just Food*. Cambridge: MIT Press.

Frijda, Nico H. 2004. "Emotions and Actions." In *Feelings and Emotions: The Amsterdam Symposium*, edited by Antony S. R. Manstead, Nico Frijda, and Agneta Fischer, 158–73. New York: Cambridge University Press.

Frye, Northrup. 1957. *Anatomy of Criticism*. Princeton: Princeton University Press.

Gayeton, Douglas. 2014. *Local: The New Face of Food and Farming in America*. New York: Harper Design.

Gecas, Viktor. 1991. "The Self-Concept as a Basis for a Theory of Motivation." In *The Self-Society Dynamic: Cognition, Emotion, and Action*, edited by Judith A. Howard and Peter L. Callero, 171–88. New York: Cambridge University Press.

Geertz, Clifford. 1973. *The Interpretation of Cultures*. New York: Basic Books.

Gody, Ron, Joyce McGarry, and Bob Tritten. 2020. "How Food Purchasing Changed in 2020—Did We Get It Right?" Michigan State University Agricultural Extension, November 20, 2020. www.canr.msu.edu.

Goldstein, Joyce. 2013. *Inside the California Food Revolution: Thirty Years That Changed Our Culinary Consciousness*. Berkeley: University of California Press.

Goranson, Jan, Rob Johnson, and Jean English. n.d. "Zone Tillage—A Reduced Tillage Option for Northern Farms." Maine Organic Farmers and Gardeners. www.mofga.org. Accessed August 12, 2021.

Grauel, Jonas. 2016. "Being Authentic or Being Responsible? Food Consumption, Morality, and the Presentation of Self." *Journal of Consumer Culture* 16 (3): 852–69.

Gray, Margaret. 2014. *Labor and the Locavore: The Making of a Comprehensive Food Ethic*. Berkeley: University of California Press.

Griffin, Matthew R., and Edward A. Frongillo. 2003. "Experiences and Perspectives of Farmers from Upstate New York Farmers' Markets." *Agriculture and Human Values* 20: 189–203.

Guthman, Julie. 2008a. "'If They Only Knew': Color Blindness and Universalism in California Alternative Food Institutions." *Professional Geographer* 60 (3): 387–97.
———. 2008b. "Neoliberalism and the Making of Food Politics in California." *Geoforum* 39: 1171–83.
Haedicke, Michael A. 2016. *Organizing Organic: Conflict and Compromise in an Emerging Market*. Stanford, CA: Stanford University Press.
Hardy, Sam A., and Gustavo Carlo. 2005. "Identity as a Source of Social Motivation." *Human Development* 48: 232–56.
Heying, Charles. 2010. *Brews to Bikes: Portland's Artisan Economy*. Portland: Ooligan Press.
Hinrichs, C. Clare. 2000. "Embeddedness and Local Food Systems: Notes on Two Types of Direct Agricultural Markets." *Journal of Rural Studies* 16: 295–303.
———. 2003. "The Practice and Politics of Food Localization." *Journal of Rural Studies* 19: 33–45.
Hinrichs, C. Clare, and Elizabeth Barham. 2007. "A Full Plate: Challenges and Opportunities in Remaking the Food System." In *Remaking the North American Food System*, edited by C. Clare Hinrichs and Thomas Lyson, 332–44. Lincoln: University of Nebraska Press.
Hinrichs, C. Clare, and Thomas Lyson, eds. 2007. *Remaking the North American Food System: Strategies for Sustainability*. Lincoln: University of Nebraska Press.
Hitlin, Steven, and Stephen Vaisey. 2013. "The New Sociology of Morality." *Annual Review of Sociology* 39: 51–68.
Hoey, Brian A. 2005. "From Pi to Pie: Moral Narratives of Noneconomic Migration and Starting Over in the Postindustrial Midwest." *Journal of Contemporary Ethnography* 34 (5): 586–624.
Holthaus, Gary. 2006. *From the Farm to the Table: What All Americans Need to Know about Agriculture*. Lexington: University of Kentucky Press.
Howard, Judith A., and Peter L. Callero, eds. 1991. *The Self-Society Dynamic: Cognition, Emotion, and Action*. New York: Cambridge University Press.
Hughes, Everett C. 1994. *On Work, Race, and the Sociological Imagination*. Chicago: University of Chicago Press.
Ignatow, Gabriel. 2009. "Why the Sociology of Morality Needs Bourdieu's Habitus." *Sociological Inquiry* 79 (1): 98–114.
Inwood, Shoshannah, Jeff S. Sharp, Richard H. Moore, and Deborah H. Stinner. 2009. "Restaurants, Chefs, and Local Foods: Insights Drawn from Application of a Diffusion of Innovation Framework." *Agriculture and Human Values* 26: 177–91.
Janssen, Brandi. 2010. "Local Food, Local Engagement: Community-Supported Agriculture in Eastern Iowa." *Culture & Agriculture* 32 (1): 4–16.
———. 2017. *Making Local Food Work: The Challenge and Opportunities of Today's Small Farmers*. Iowa City: University of Iowa Press.
Jasper, James. 1988. "The Emotions of Protest: Affective and Reactive Emotions in and around Social Movements." *Sociological Forum* 13 (3): 397–424.

———. 2011. "Emotions and Social Movements: Twenty Years of Theory and Research." *Annual Review of Sociology* 37: 285–303.
Johnston, Josee, and Shyon Baumann. 2007. "Democracy versus Distinction: A Study of Omnivorousness in Gourmet Food Writing." *American Journal of Sociology* 113 (1): 171.
———. 2009. "Tension in the Kitchen: Explicit and Implicit Politics in the Gourmet Foodscape." *Sociologica* 3 (1): 1–29.
———. 2015 [2010]. *Foodies: Democracy and Distinction in the Gourmet Foodscape*. New York: Routledge.
Jordan, Jennifer A. 2015. *Edible Memory: The Lure of Heirloom Tomatoes and Other Forgotten Foods*. Chicago: University of Chicago Press.
Kaltoff, Permille. 1999. "Values about Nature in Organic Farming Practice and Knowledge." *Sociologia Ruralis* 39 (1): 39–53.
Keller, Suzanne. 2003. *Community: Pursuing the Dream, Living the Reality*. Princeton: Princeton University Press.
Kennedy, Emily Huddart, Josee Johnston, and John R. Parkins. 2017. "Small-p Politics: How Pleasurable, Convivial and Pragmatic Political Ideals Influence Engagement in Eat-Local Initiatives." *British Journal of Sociology* 69 (3): 1–21.
Kessler, Anna, John R. Parkins, and Emily Huddart Kennedy. 2016. "Environmental Harms and 'the Good Farmer': Conceptualizing Discourses of Environmental Sustainability in the Beef Industry." *Rural Sociology* 8 (2): 172–93.
Kessler, John. 2013. "The Upstart Cattleman." In *Best Food Writing, 2013*, edited by Holly Hughes, 150–59. Philadelphia: Da Capo.
Kingsolver, Barbara. 2007. *Animal, Vegetable, Miracle*. New York: HarperCollins.
Kloppenburg, Jack, Jr., John Hendrickson, and G. W. Stevenson. 1996. "Coming into the Foodshed." *Agriculture and Human Values* 13 (3): 33–42.
———. 2000. "Tasting Food, Tasting Sustainability: Defining the Attributes of an Alternative Food System with Competent, Ordinary People." *Human Organization* 59 (2): 177–86.
Kunda, Gideon. 2006. *Engineering Culture: Control and Commitment in a High-Tech Corporation*. Rev. ed. Philadelphia: Temple University Press.
Lane, Christel. 2014. *The Cultivation of Taste: Chefs and the Organization of Fine Dining*. Oxford, UK: Oxford University Press.
Lapping, Mark B. 2004. "Towards the Recovery of the Local in the Globalizing Food System: The Role of Alternative Agricultural and Food Models in the US." *Ethics, Place and Environment* 7 (3): 141–50.
Lee, Roger. 2000. "Shelter from the Storm: Geographies of Regard in the Worlds of Horticultural Consumption and Production." *Geoforum* 31: 137–57.
Leschziner, Vanina. 2010. "Cooking Logics: Cognition and Reflexivity in the Culinary Field." In *Globalization, Food, and Social Identities in the Pacific Region*, edited by James Farrar, 1–15. Tokyo: Sophia University Institute of Comparative Culture.

Lively, Kathryn J., and Brian Powell. 2006. "Emotional Expression at Work and at Home: Domain, Status, or Individual Characteristics." *Social Psychology Quarterly* 69 (1): 17–38.

Low, Sarah, et al. 2015. "Trends in US Local and Regional Food Systems." US Department of Agriculture, Economic Research Service. www.ams.usda.gov.

Lynch, Meghan, and Audrey Giles. 2013. "Let Them Eat Organic Cake: Discourses in Sustainable Food Initiatives." *Food, Culture & Society* 16 (3): 479–93.

Macias, Thomas. 2008. "Working toward a Just, Equitable, and Local Food System: The Social Impacts of Community-Based Agriculture." *Social Science Quarterly* 89 (5): 1086–1101.

MacKendrick, Norah. 2018. *Better Safe Than Sorry: How Consumers Navigate Exposure to Everyday Toxics*. Berkeley: University of California Press.

Manstead, Antony S. R., Nico Frijda, and Agneta Fischer, eds. 2004. *Feelings and Emotions: The Amsterdam Symposium*. New York: Cambridge University Press.

Mars, Matthew M., and Hope Jensen Schau. 2017. "Institutional Entrepreneurship and Negotiation and Blending of Multiple Logics in the Southern Arizona Local Food System." *Agriculture and Human Values* 34: 407–22.

Mathews, Holly F. 1992. "The Directive Force of Morality Tales in a Mexican Community." In *Human Motives and Cultural Models*, edited by Roy D'Andrade and Claudia Strauss, 127–63. New York: Cambridge University Press.

Mayer, Frederick. 2014. *Narrative Politics*. New York: Oxford University Press.

McInerney, Paul-Brian. 2014. *From Social Movement to Moral Market: How the Circuit Riders Sparked an IT Revolution and Created a Technology Market*. Stanford, CA: Stanford University Press.

McKibben, Bill. 2006. "A Grand Experiment." In *Best Food Writing, 2006*, edited by Holly Hughes, 10–18. Philadelphia: Da Capo.

———. 2007. *Deep Economy: The Wealth of Communities and the Durable Future*. New York: Times Books, Henry Holt.

McNamee, Thomas. 2007. *Alice Waters and Chez Panisse: The Romantic, Impractical, Often Eccentric, Ultimately Brilliant Making of a Food Revolution*. New York: Penguin.

Michaelson, Christopher. 2009. "Meaningful Work and Moral Worth." *Business & Professional Ethics Journal* 28 (1–4): 27–48.

Mikulak, Michael. 2013. *The Politics of the Pantry*. Montreal: McGill-Queen's University Press.

Mills, Trudy, and Sheryl Kleinman. 1988. "Emotions, Reflexivity, and Action: An Interactionist Analysis." *Social Forces* 66 (4): 1009–27.

Monroe, Kristen Renwick. 2001. "Morality and a Sense of the Self: The Importance of Identity and Categorization for Moral Action." *Journal of Political Science* 45 (3): 491–507.

Morgan, Caitlin. 2020. "Commensality in Crisis." *Gastronomica* 30: 46–47.

Nabhan, Gary Paul. 2002. *Coming Home to Eat: The Pleasures and Politics of Local Foods*. New York: Norton.

Nelson, Paul, Mary A. Beckie, and Naomi T. Krogman. 2017. "The 'Locavore' Chef in Alberta: A Situated Social Practice Analysis." *Food, Culture & Society* 20 (3): 503–24.

Obach, Brian. 2015. *Organic Struggle: The Sustainable Agriculture Movement in the United States*. Cambridge: MIT Press.

Ocejo, Richard C. 2018. *Masters of Craft: Old Jobs in the New Urban Economy*. Princeton: Princeton University Press.

Offer, Avner. 1997. "Between the Gift and the Market: The Economy of Regard." *Economic History Review, n.s.,* 50 (3): 450–76.

Ostrom, Marcia. 2006. "Everyday Meanings of 'Local Food': Views from Home and Field." *Community Development* 37 (1): 65–78.

Papaoikonomou, Eleni, and Matias Ginieis. 2016. "Putting a Farmer's Face on Food: Governance and the Producer-Consumer Relationship in the Local Food System." *Agriculture and Human Values* 34: 53–67.

Parkins, Wendy, and Geoffrey Craig. 2009. "Culture and the Politics of Alternative Food Networks." *Food, Culture & Society* 12 (1): 78–103.

Parks, Melissa M., and Christine Anderson Brekken. 2019. "Cosmovisions and Farming Praxis: An Investigation of Conventional and Alternative Farmers along the Willamette River." *Culture, Agriculture, Food and Environment* 41 (1): 34–44.

Paxson, Heather. 2012. *The Life of Cheese: Crafting Food and Value in America*. Berkeley: University of California Press.

Pecoraro, Maria Grazia, and Outi Uusitalo. 2014. "Conflicting Values of Ethical Consumption in Diverse Worlds—A Cultural Approach." *Journal of Consumer Culture* 14 (1): 45–65.

Pole, Antoinette, and Margaret Gray. 2012. "Farming Alone? What's Up with the 'C' in Community Supported Agriculture." *Agriculture and Human Values* 30: 85–100.

Pollan, Michael. 2006a. "Eat Your View." *On the Table* (blog), *New York Times*, May 17, 2006. https://michaelpollan.com.

———. 2006b. *The Omnivore's Dilemma: A Natural History of Four Meals*. New York: Penguin.

———. 2008. *In Defense of Food: An Eater's Manifesto*. New York: Penguin.

———. 2010. "The Food Movement Rising." *New York Review of Books*, May 20, 2010. https://michaelpollan.com.

Polletta, Francesca. 2006. *It Was Like a Fever: Storytelling in Protest and Politics*. Chicago: University of Chicago Press.

Ponte, Stefano. 2016. "Convention Theory in the Anglophone Agro-Food Literature: Past, Present, and Future." *Journal of Rural Studies* 44: 12–23.

Press, Melea, and Eric J. Arnould. 2011. "Legitimating Community Supported Agriculture through American Pastoralist Ideology." *Journal of Consumer Culture* 11 (2): 168–94.

Qazi, Joan A., and Theresa L. Selfa. 2005. "The Politics of Building Alternative Agro-Food Networks in the Belly of the Beast." *Food, Culture, & Society* 8 (1): 45–72.

Rao, Hayagreeva. 2009. *Market Rebels: How Activists Make or Break Radical Innovations*. Princeton: Princeton University Press.

Robinson, Jennifer Meta, and James Robert Farmer. 2017. *Selling Local: Why Local Food Movements Matter*. Bloomington: University of Indiana Press.

Ross, Nancy. 2006. "How Civic Is It? Success Stories in Locally Focused Agriculture in Maine." *Renewable Agriculture and Food Systems* 21 (2): 114–23.

Ryder, Tracey, and Carole Topalian. 2010. *Edible: A Celebration of Local Foods*. Hoboken, NJ: John Wiley.

Sage, Colin. 2003. "Social Embeddedness and Relations of Regard: Alternative 'Good Food' Networks in South-West Ireland." *Journal of Rural Studies* 19: 47–60.

Sayer, Andrew. 2005a. "Class, Moral Worth and Recognition." *Sociology* 39 (5): 947–63.

———. 2005b. *The Moral Significance of Class*. Cambridge: Cambridge University Press.

———. 2011. *Why Things Matter to People: Social Science, Values, and Ethical Life*. Cambridge: Cambridge University Press.

Scheff, Thomas J. 1988. "Shame and Conformity: The Deference-Emotion System." *American Review of Sociology* 53: 395–406.

Schnell, Steven M. 2013. "Food Miles, Local Eating, and Community Supported Agriculture: Putting Local Food in Its Place." *Agriculture and Human Values* 30: 615–28.

Schor, Juliet B., and Craig J. Thompson, eds. 2014. *Sustainable Lifestyles and the Quest for Plenitude*. New Haven: Yale University Press.

Schrank, Zach. 2014. "Cultivating Localization through Commodity De-Fetishization: Contours of Authenticity and the Pursuit of Transparency in the Local Organic Agrarian Food Market." In *Food and Everyday Life*, edited by Thomas M. Conroy, 147–71. New York: Lexington Books.

Schwalbe, Michael. 1991. "Social Structure and the Moral Self." In *The Self-Society Dynamic: Cognition, Emotion, and Action*, edited by Judith A. Howard and Peter L. Callero, 281–304. New York: Cambridge University Press.

Shisler, Rebecca C., and Joshua Sbicca. 2019. "Agriculture as Carework: The Contradictions of Performing Femininity in a Male-Dominated Occupation." *Society & Natural Resources* 32 (8): 875–92.

Simpson, Ruth, Natasha Slutskaya, Patricia Lewis, and Heather Höpfl. 2012. "Introducing Dirty Work, Concepts and Identities." In *Dirty Work: Concepts and Identities*, edited by Ruth Simpson, Natasha Slutskaya, Patricia Lewis, and Heather Höpfl. New York: Palgrave Macmillan.

Smith, Christian. 2009. *Moral, Believing Animals*. Chicago: University of Chicago Press.

Smith, Philip. 2005. *Why War? The Cultural Logic of Iraq, the Gulf War, and Suez*. Chicago: University of Chicago Press.

Stamer, Naja Buono. 2018. "Moral Conventions in Food Consumption and Their Relationship to Consumers' Social Background." *Journal of Consumer Culture* 18 (1): 202–22.

Stets, Jan E., and Michael J. Carter. 2011. "The Moral Self: Applying Identity Theory." *Social Psychology Quarterly* 74 (2): 192–215.

———. 2012. "A Theory of the Self for the Sociology of Morality." *American Sociological Review* 77 (1): 120–40.

Stevenson, G. W., Kathryn Ruhf, Sharon Lezberg, and Kate Clancy. 2007. "Warrior, Builder, and Weaver Work: Strategies for Changing the Food System." In *Remaking the North American Food System*, edited by C. Clare Hinrichs and Thomas Lyson, 33–62. Lincoln: University of Nebraska Press.

Stock, Paul V. 2007. "Good Farmers as Reflexive Producers: An Examination of Family Organic Farmers in the US Midwest." *Sociologia Ruralis* 47 (2): 83–102.

———. 2021. "Food Utopias, (Mature) Care, and Hope." *International Journal of Agriculture & Food* 27 (2): 89–107.

Strasburg, Michael. 2020. "After Covid-19 Disruptions, Hog Industry Encourages Consumers to Purchase Pork." SW Newsmedia, June 8, 2020. www.swnewsmedia.com.

Strauss, Claudia. 1992. "Models and Motives." In *Human Motives and Cultural Models*, edited by Roy D'Andrade and Claudia Strauss, 1–20. New York: Cambridge University Press.

Sutherland, Lee-Ann, and Ika Darnhofer. 2012. "Of Organic Farmers and 'Good Farmers': Changing Habitus in Rural England." *Journal of Rural Studies* 28: 232–40.

Swidler, Ann. 1986. "Culture in Action: Symbols and Strategies." *American Sociological Review* 51 (2): 273–86.

———. 2001. *Talk of Love: How Culture Matters*. Chicago: University of Chicago Press.

———. 2008. "Comment on Stephen Vaisey's 'Socrates, Skinner and Aristotle: Three Ways of Thinking about Culture in Action.'" *Sociological Forum* 23 (3): 614–18.

Tavory, Ivo. 2011. "The Question of Moral Action: A Formalist Position." *Sociological Theory* 29 (4): 272–93.

Thoits, Peggy, 1989. "The Sociology of Emotions." *Annual Review of Sociology* 15: 317–42.

Thompson, Craig J., and Gokcen Coskuner-Balli. 2007a. "Countervailing Market Responses to Corporate Co-optation and the Ideological Recruitment of Consumption Communities." *Journal of Consumer Research* 34: 135–52.

———. 2007b. "Enchanting Ethical Consumerism: The Case of Community Supported Agriculture." *Journal of Consumer Culture* 7 (3): 275–303.

Thompson, Craig J., and Melea Press. 2014. "How Community Supported Agriculture Facilitates Reembedding and Reterritorializing Practices of Sustainable Consumption." In *Sustainable Lifestyles and the Quest for Plenitude*, edited by Juliet B. Schor and Craig J. Thompson, 125–47. New Haven: Yale University Press.

Thompson, Paul B. 2010. *The Agrarian Vision: Sustainability and Environmental Ethics*. Lexington: University of Kentucky Press.

Trivette, Shawn A. 2015. "How Local Is Local? Determining the Boundaries of Local Food in Practice." *Agriculture and Human Values* 32: 475–90.

———. 2017. "Invoices on Scraps of Paper: Trust and Reciprocity in Local Food Systems." *Agriculture and Human Values* 34: 529–42.

Tropp, Debra. 2014. "Why Local Food Matters: The Rising Importance of Locally-Grown Food in the US Food System: A National Perspective." USDA report. www.ers.usda.gov.

Trubek, Amy B. 2008. *The Taste of Place: A Cultural Journey into Terroir*. Berkeley: University of California Press.
Turner, Jonathan H., and Jan E. Stets. 2006. "Sociological Theories of Human Emotions." *Annual Review of Sociology* 32: 25–52.
Vaisey, Stephen. 2009. "Motivation and Justification: A Dual-Process Model of Culture in Action." *American Journal of Sociology* 114 (6): 1675–1715.
VanWinkle, Tony N. 2017. "Savor the Earth to Save It! The Pedagogy of Sustainable Pleasure and Relational Ecology in a Place-Based Public Culinary Culture." *Food and Foodways* 25 (1): 40–57.
Weber, Klaus, Kathryn L. Heinze, and Michaela DeSoucey. 2008. "Forage for Thought: Mobilizing Codes in the Movement for Grass Fed Meat and Dairy Products." *Administrative Science Quarterly* 53: 529–67.
Weiler, Anelyse M., Gerardo Otero, and Hannah Wittman. 2016. "Rock Stars and Bad Apples: Moral Economies of Alternative Food Networks and Precarious Farm Work Regimes." *Antipode* 48 (4): 1140–62.
Wells, Betty L., Shelly Gradwell, and Rhonda Yoder. 2002. "Growing Food, Growing Community: Community Supported Agriculture in Rural Iowa." In *Food in the USA: A Reader*, edited by Carole Counihan, 401–8. New York: Routledge.
Westervelt, Eric. 2020a. "As Food Supply Chain Breaks Down, Farm-to-Door CSAs Take Off." NPR, May 10, 2020. www.npr.org
———. 2020b. "During Pandemic, Community Supported Agriculture Sees Membership Spike." NPR, May 14, 2020. www.npr.org.
White, Hayden. 1973. *Metahistory: The Historical Imagination in Nineteenth-Century Europe*. Baltimore: Johns Hopkins University Press.
Winchester, Daniel. 2008. "Embodying the Faith: Religious Practice and the Making of a Muslim Moral Habitus." *Social Forces* 86 (4): 1753–80.
———. 2016. "A Hunger for God: Embodied Metaphor as Cultural Cognition in Action." *Social Forces* 95 (2): 585–606.
Winchester, Daniel, and Kyle D. Green. 2019. "Talking Your Self into It: How and When Accounts Shape Motivation for Action." *Sociological Theory* 37 (3): 257–81.
Woods, Timothy, Matthew Ernst, and Debra Tropp. 2017. "Community Supported Agriculture: New Models for Changing Markets." USDA report. www.ers.usda.gov.
Worster, Donald. 1984. *Nature's Economy: A History of Ecological Ideas*. New York: Cambridge University Press.
Wuthnow, Robert. 1987. *Meaning and Moral Order: Explorations in Cultural Analysis*. Berkeley: University of California Press.
———. 1996. *Poor Richard's Principle: Recovering the American Dream through the Moral Dimension of Work, Business, and Money*. Princeton: Princeton University Press.
Zelizer, Viviana. 1979. *Morals and Markets: The Development of Life Insurance in the United States*. New York: Columbia University Press.

INDEX

Ackerman-Leist, Philip, 174n2
action. *See* social action
agriculture. *See* community-supported agriculture; farmers; industrial agriculture and food systems; local and alternative food systems; meat producers; regenerative agriculture; *specific topics*
agritourism, 130, 142, 151
alternative food networks. *See* local and alternative food systems; *specific topics*
Anderson, Mark, 19–20
animals: husbandry pride in care of, 36, 49, 64, 65, 89; industrial agriculture exploitation of, 14; meat producers' ethical approach to, 56–57, 64; pioneer stories on treatment of, 21. *See also* meat producers; nose-to-tail cooking
artisanal products and producers, 37; increase in, 6, 7; local food definition and, 10; McKibben on, 18
authenticity, 47–48, 51, 53, 157, 165n6. *See also* trust and transparency
autonomy, 10, 52, 168n61

Barber, Dan, 78, 92–93, 171n31
Barham, Elizabeth, 151
Barnard, Alex, 48, 168n75
Baumann, Shyon, 11, 14
Beckie, Mary, 75
beef production. *See* meat producers
beekeeping, 42–43
Beingessner, Naomi, 46
Bell, Michael, 90
Berry, Wendell, 21, 96
biodiversity, 4, 9; farmers promotion of and commitment to, 11, 19, 30, 42, 44, 46, 54, 60, 67, 126, 128, 160; regenerative agriculture and, 101, 172n8
Bittman, Mark, 14
Bourdieu, Pierre, 32, 169n79
breweries, 37
Brown, Keith, 173n19
Bruce, Analena, 46, 62, 170n16, 170n20

California, farm-to-table movement, 9, 74–75
Canadian local farmers, 46, 172n7
capitalistic markets: community building obstacles with influence of, 154, 155; ethical norms erosion in, 103; farmers views on, 42, 51, 95–96; food as commodity in, 3, 7, 103; moral order in, 29, 171n2; norms and normativity, 29, 95–96, 103
care work, 4, 165n6
Carson, Rachel, 21, 41
cattle ranchers. *See* meat producers
cheesemakers, 7, 37, 48, 49; chefs' relationships with, 9, 114, 157; cooperative norm of, 107–8, 146; food safety regulations and, 90; legacy/returning farmers as, 62, 69–70; pandemic impact for, 145–46; pioneer stories on, 23; on transparency and trust, 104–5
chefs, 37; aesthetics, taste, and quality as motivation for, 74–76, 77, 80, 82–84; apprenticeships for, 78; commitment to local farmers over profit, 82; on community building, 22, 80; consumer education by, 76–77, 121–22, 131–33; cooperative norm for, 107; CSA relationships built with, 113–15; environmental consciousness of, 79; farmer/supplier relationship cultivation for, 9, 75, 76, 77, 81–84, 114–15, 126–27, 157, 171n31; on food hubs, 135–36, 149–50; forager relationships with, 76, 77, 114, 157; on lack of infrastructure, 135–36; on local food commitment over organic, 80–82; meat producer challenges with choices of, 117–19; moral codes for, 74–84; mutual support, 157; nose-to-tail cooking practices of, 75, 79, 80, 121–22; pandemic community service of, 147–48; pandemic opportunities for, 149–50; pioneer stories on locavore, 16, 22; seasonal foods focus for, 9; on sustainability, 78–79, 80, 121–22; taste and quality of local food importance for, 74–76, 77, 80, 82–84; trust in relationships with, 83, 114–15; Alice Waters, 9, 14, 75, 78, 171n31
Chef's Table, 92–93

189

climate change, 3, 14, 56
Collins, Randall, 36, 175n24
Coming Home to Eat (Nabhan), 16–18
community building, 10; challenges with, 112–13, 151, 153–55; chefs on, 22, 80; commitment to, 3, 26, 43–44; contemporary pastoralism and, 168n61; CSAs focus on, 108–13; economics and self-interest as obstacles to, 154, 155; farmers' markets and, 4, 47, 103; "good farmer" ethics around, 47; joy and belonging with, 110–11; legacy/returning farmers on, 71; local food narratives on, 14; local food support relation to, 3, 9; local market norms around, 108–15, 172n10; as new farmers motivation, 58; pandemic and, 147–48, 150; shared experiences role in, 160; skill set for farmers, 155
community gardens, 5–6, 10
community-supported agriculture (CSA), 37; beekeeping and, 42–43; challenges sustaining, 136–37; chef and restaurant relationships fostered with, 113–15; community building and consumer relationship focus with, 108–13; community building challenges for, 112–13, 153; community events at, 109–10, 143–44; consumer education practice, 120–21; cooperation among owners of, 106–7, 152; ethics behind, 4; farmer motivations, 9, 25, 45; farm size for, 41–42, 95–97; increase in, 6; internships, 51–52, 84, 94–95, 96, 111; for legacy and returning farmers, 61, 62; local food definition and, 10; member motivations, 111; pandemic impacts for, 40, 140, 143–44; profits, 42; sliding scale practices for, 97–98, 157; soil fertility challenges and, 96–97; subscriber and sweat-equity models for, 96, 108–9; transformative experiences for farmers in, 51
consumer: creating steady support from, 153–55, 165n1; direct-to-consumer market for, 5, 135, 147; education, 76–77, 88, 121–22, 130–33; education around scale and prices, 120–21, 131–32; moral market motivations and participation of, 4, 35, 91, 92; nose-to-tail education for, 88, 121–22; seasonal foods understanding of, 130; socioeconomics and race of local food, 97–98, 137–39, 157, 169n97. *See also* health, of food and consumers
consumer relationships, 5, 10, 135; emotional feedback loop with, 71–72, 159–60; importance of, 3, 92, 108; transparency and trust fostered in, 3, 4, 15, 16, 104–5, 114–15
conventional agriculture and food systems: alternative farmers' values contrasted with farmers in, 45–46; farmers shift from, 69; food as commodity in, 3, 7, 80, 103; "good" criteria for, 29–30; health-related fears around, 7–8; legacy/returning farmers' use of, 65–66, 88–89; local food market competing with, 91–92, 99; market niche creation challenges within, 91–92; moral order in, 29–30; small-scale local costs, risk, and profits contrasted with, 6; supermarket prices and, 122–23, 137; supermarkets in, 15–16, 120, 122–23, 137; three pillars of, 7; as villain in pioneer stories, 23. *See also* industrial agriculture and food systems
cooperation, 151; of cheesemakers, 107–8, 146; CSAs, with one another, 106–7, 152; infrastructure creation through, 152–53, 174n4; during pandemic, 146; restaurant practices and attitudes around, 107–8
corporate food production. *See* conventional agriculture and food systems; industrial agriculture and food systems
Coskuner-Balli, Gokcen, 53
costs: challenges for local food producers, 88, 89, 165n1; for conventional compared with small-scale local producers, 6; of eating local and seasonally, 19
COVID-19 (pandemic): agritourism during, 142; challenges and opportunities during, 40, 125, 127, 128, 129, 139–50; cheesemakers during, 145–46; community building during, 147–48, 150; cooperation for success during, 146; CSAs and, 40, 140, 143–44; direct-to-consumer pivots during, 147; farmers business closing during, 128, 129; innovation during, 142, 144–45, 146, 147; local food assessments prior to, 129–39; meat producers impacted by, 139–40, 142; profits during, 142–43; restaurants during, 127, 139, 141, 147–50
CSA. *See* community-supported agriculture
customer. *See* consumer
customer relationships. *See* consumer relationships

dairy farmers, 51–52; legacy/returning farmers and, 63–64, 69–70; New York abundance

INDEX | 191

of, 6; pandemic impact on, 139, 141. *See also* cheesemakers
DeLind, Laura, 9, 153–54, 155, 175n13
DeSoucey, Michaela, 47–48, 171n21
direct-to-consumer market, 5, 135, 147. *See also* community-supported agriculture; farmers' markets
distribution. *See* infrastructure
dumpster divers, 48

economic sociology, 29
emotional insights, 69, 171n23
emotions: as cues to social action, 35–36, 40, 69; farming motivation and "emotional insights," 69; food writing triggering, 13–14, 23–24; greenhorn farmers entry into farming relation to, 52–54; identity relationship with, 73, 86, 158–59; interaction ritual chains and, 175n24; legacy/returning farmers motivations and, 71–72; local food producers commitment relation to, 52–54, 71–72, 85; morality and social action relation to, 3, 27–32, 35–37, 40, 54, 85, 155–60, 168n75, 169n91, 169n94, 175n24; physical acts of farming impact on, 159; with pioneer stories, 23–24; ritual and, 53–54; short-lived energy from, 36
environmental consciousness, 41; of chefs, 79; chefs on taste and quality priority over, 75; climate change concerns and, 3, 14, 56; farmers morality around, 34, 45–46; food miles and, 8, 14; local food movement and, 7, 24; local food narratives on, 14, 18–19; new farmers motivations around, 54–58, 60–61; organic food market and, 8; pork production and, 18–19; sustainability role in, 45–46; working by hand to avoid fossil fuels and, 43, 98–99. *See also* stewardship

fair trade, 35, 154, 173n19
family: legacy farmers focus on, 62–63, 69–70, 170n20; work load balance with, 26, 97
farmer cooperatives, 174n4
farmers, 37, 166n18; on aesthetics of produce over soil health, 54–55; alternative direct-to-consumer marketing practices, 135; beekeeping and honey production for, 42–43; biodiversity promotion and commitment of, 11, 19, 30, 42, 44, 46, 54, 60, 67, 126, 128, 160; business failure during pandemic, 128, 129; on capitalist markets, 42, 51, 95–96;

chefs cultivating relationships with, 9, 75, 77, 81–84, 114–15, 126–27, 157, 171n31; community building skill set, 155; connections to natural world, 26, 50; consumer relationships and emotional feedback loop for, 71–72, 159–60; costs as obstacles for, 165n1; farm size and expansion limits for, 95–97, 99, 100–101, 115–19, 152; "good," 34, 45, 62, 64, 70, 156, 160; greenhorn (new), 41, 49–61, 170n1, 170n16; high-end organic/sustainable, 45; honey production for, 42–43; industrial agriculture exploitation of, 14; moral codes for legacy and returning, 61–74, 170n20; moral codes for new, 49–61; morality around health of food and consumers, 34, 46, 123–24, 156; moral significance in work of, 33–34, 43–44, 47–48, 123–24, 128–29; motivations, 26–27, 48, 54–58, 60–61, 71–72, 99, 126, 127–28; mutual support, 157; network needed for distribution, 151–52; sharing resources with other farmers, 106–7; on tangible results of labor, 53, 54, 63, 70–71; transformative experiences for, 44, 50, 52–53, 61, 73, 85–86, 159; values in alternative compared with conventional food systems, 45–46; working by hand to avoid fossil fuels, 43, 98–99; work load sustainability for, 95–96. *See also* community-supported agriculture; dairy farmers; greenhorn (new) farmers; legacy and returning farmers; meat producers; *specific topics*
farmers' markets, 37; aesthetics of produce at, 54–55; community building and, 4, 47, 103; consumer education at, 132; cooperative norms at, 106, 108; CSA creation in response to low sales at, 41; increase since 1994, 5; local food definition and, 10; moral economy of, 103; pandemic impact on, 144–45; rules for avoiding competition at, 106, 173n13; state-level policy support for, 6; trust and transparency norms for, 102, 104, 115
farmland preservation, 9, 11, 14, 44, 151. *See also* soil health/fertility
farm size: CSAs, 41–42, 95–97; government policies and, 1–2; limits and obstacles, 1, 2, 6, 95–97, 100–101, 115–19, 152; work load balance with, 96, 97
farm-to-table, 9, 74–76, 77, 88, 90, 130, 149
Farrell, Justin, 25, 28–29, 167n54
Ferguson, Priscilla Parkhurst, 11
fields, Bourdieu concept of, 32

Fine, Gary Alan, 29, 30, 74
Fletcher, Amber, 46
flooding, 2
food, as care work, 4, 165n6
food, as commodity, 3, 7, 80, 103
food hubs, 10, 131; chef on, 135–36, 149–50; definition of, 174n3; failure of, 134, 153; grants for development of, 152; growth from 1994 to 2019, 5; lack of, 6
foodie culture, 7, 9, 11, 22
food justice. *See* justice
food memoirs: *Coming Home to Eat* (Nabhan), 16–18; "A Grand Experiment" (McKibben), 18–19, 20, 56; influence of, 20, 24; "Miles to Go before I Eat" (Anderson), 19–20; transformation of self shown in, 19, 20
food miles: average, for Americans, 15, 18; environmental impact of, 8, 14; health impact of, 9; hundred-mile diet and, 16, 19, 22
food quality. *See* taste and quality
food safety, 7–8, 10, 14, 90
food shortages, 152–53
Food & Wine, 22, 166n39
food writing/journalism: champions of local, organic, and sustainable agriculture in, 14; emotions and action triggered with, 13–14, 23–24; in foodie culture, 11; impacts of, 24; morality tales and, 25; moral vision compared to reality in, 25–26; Pollan, 14, 15–16, 24, 52; production and consumption practices impacted by, 11–12; sources for research, 166n39; themes common in alternative/local, 14, 18. *See also* food memoirs; pioneer stories; taste and quality
foragers, 37; chefs' relationships with, 9, 16, 22, 76, 77, 114, 157; community-supported, 22; moral code for, 29
Fourcade, Marion, 29

garlic farmer, 125–28
gastronomy, 11
Geertz, Clifford, 28
genetically modified crops, 128–29, 166n18
Georgia, 21–22
globalization, 7
"good farmer": health of food and consumers role for, 46, 156; morality and ethics, 34, 45–49, 62, 64, 68, 70, 156, 160
government policies, 37; food security and, 26; funding for local food market, 152; on health and food choices, 165n1; small-scale local farming and, 1–2; state-level, 5–6
grain production, 1, 4, 17, 18, 62, 89
"A Grand Experiment" (McKibben), 18–19, 20, 56
grass-fed meat producers, 10, 48, 57, 67, 80, 99–101, 171n21
greenhorn (new) farmers, 41, 170n1; apprenticeships for, 51, 59; college background for, 49, 50, 51, 59, 61; educational resources for, 100, 101; elements of entry for, 52–53; environmental consciousness of, 54–58, 60–61; internships as pathway for, 50, 51–52; learning curves, 87–88, 94–95; moral codes for, 49–61, 73; as opportunists turned ethical farmers, 57–58; social class and social networks role for, 59–60, 170n16; on tangible results of labor, 53, 54; transformative experiences impact for, 44, 50, 52–53, 61, 85–86
grocery stores, local-focused: closing of, 6; organic, 10, 134–35. *See also* supermarkets, conventional

habitus: Bourdieu defining, 32, 169n79; farmers moral, 61, 84–85, 159
health, of food and consumers, 9, 10, 14; conventional food systems distrust around, 7–8; farmers' moral sentiments around, 34, 46, 123–24, 156; food memoirs on locavore diet impact on, 18–20; "good farmer" ethics around, 46, 156; legacy/returning farmers concerns for, 62–63, 66–67, 69, 71, 72; organic pesticides and, 55; Pollan on local food impacts on, 15–16
Healy, Kieran, 29
Heinze, Kathryn, 47–48, 171n21
Hell's Kitchen, 74
Hinrichs, C. Clare, 91, 151
Holthaus, Gary, 46
home gardens, business from, 22
honesty. *See* trust and transparency
honey production, 42–43
hundred-mile diet, 16, 19, 20, 22
husbandry, 36, 49, 64, 65, 89

identity: action and emotions relation to, 169n91; emotions relationship with, 73, 86; ethical social action relation to preservation of, 31–32, 37, 158; farmers seeking authenticity of, 47–48, 51, 53, 158; "good" farmer, 34,

45, 47–48, 62, 64, 70, 156, 157, 160; morality and moral codes relation to self, 34–35, 36–37, 47–48, 156, 157–59; new farmers on work relation to, 52; stories' role in individual and national, 13

In Defense of Food (Pollan), 15–16

industrial agriculture and food systems: activism challenging, historically, 7; consolidation of, 17; critiques of, 14–17, 21, 41; lack of trust and transparency in, 7–8, 17

infrastructure, 3; chefs on lack of, 135–36; convenience and, 136–37; cooperative approach to, 152–53, 174n4; insufficiencies, 135–36, 153, 174n2; issues for local and alternative food systems, 1, 6, 39, 91, 117, 131, 133–34; pandemic highlighting weaknesses in, 153; types of local food, 10. *See also* food hubs

interaction ritual chains, 175n24

Johnston, Josee, 11, 14

journalism, food. *See* food writing/journalism

justice: commitments to, 4, 30, 60, 96, 97–98, 156, 157; food security and, 97–98, 137–38

Keller, Thomas, 78
Kessler, John, 21–22
Kingsolver, Barbara, 14, 56
Kloppenburg, Jack, 103
Krogman, Naomi, 75

Lapping, Mark, 7
lay normativity, 27
legacy and returning farmers: on biodiversity preservation, 67, 126, 128; cheesemakers as, 62, 69–70; conventional agriculture practices of, 65–66, 88–89; health of food and consumers importance for, 62–63, 66–67, 69, 71, 72; joy of job for, 70–71; lifestyle and family goals for, 62–63, 69–70, 170n20; markets for, 61–62; moral codes for, 61–74, 125–26, 157, 170n20; second jobs for, 62; on shift from conventional to alternative practices, 69; on social good of their work, 65; stewardship importance for, 62–63, 64, 65, 126; on sustainability, 64, 65, 67–68, 69

local and alternative food systems, 37; availability of, 31; challenges for entering and sustaining, 1–2, 87–101, 115–24, 151–53, 165n1; classifying, 5, 9–10, 166n18; climate change impacted with, 3, 14, 56; conventional food market competition for, 91–92, 99; "dirty work" in, 38; farmers success in high-end, 45; farmers values in conventional contrasted with, 45–46; farm size limits and obstacles for, 95–97, 100–101; moral order guiding, 3, 4–5, 30, 33, 38, 39; networking challenges and needs for, 151–53; optimistic views of, 129–30; pathways into, factors behind, 49; pioneer stories heroes creating, 20, 21–22; prepandemic assessments of, 129–39; proximity and space in determination of, 9–10; risk and uncertainty for producers in, 2, 6, 38, 87, 90; shared values in, 10–11, 38, 45; trust and transparency fostered in, 3, 4, 10, 15, 16, 89, 91, 102–3, 104–5, 114–15, 158; USDA report in 2015 on importance, 5; Walmart approach to, 173n22. *See also specific topics*

local food, future of: assessments prior to pandemic, 129–39; commensality and, 160; goals and needs for, 131, 151; networking needs for, 151–53; provisional conclusions about, 150–55

local food movement, 92; criticisms of, 26; food writing and stories behind, 11–27; history, 7; moral vision compared to reality in, 25–26, 30; pathways into, 49, 85; populations excluded from, 26; rationales and appeals underlying, 24, 38

Local Harvest, 6

local market creation and norms: buy local campaigns/initiatives for, 8–9, 119, 151; cooperation role in, 105–8, 146, 151, 152–53, 174n4; education of public in, 105; farm size limits and challenges in, 1, 115–19, 152; meeting market demand approach to, 133; moral economy of, 103; networking needs for, 151–53; relationships and community building in, 108–15, 172n10; socioeconomics and race of consumer relation to, 97–98, 137–39, 157, 169n97; stable market and customer base challenges in, 165n1; trade in, 107; trust and transparency in, 102, 104–5, 108, 115, 123, 158; Walmart competition and, 173n22. *See also* moral market

markets. *See* capitalistic markets; farmers' markets; local market creation and norms; moral market

Mayer, Frederick, 12, 23
McKibben, Bill, 18–19, 20, 56
meat processors, 87; lack of local, 134; small scale farms challenges with, 116–17

meat producers, 37–38; antibiotic use for, 89; authenticity commitment from, 48; carrying capacity concerns for, 99; chefs meat choices as challenges for, 117–19; consumer education from, 88; consumers ability/desire to pay prices of, 119–21; educational resources for, 100; ethical approach to animals, 56–57, 64; farm size limits and challenges for, 99, 100–101, 116–18; on fulfillment in work, 63; grass-fed, 10, 48, 57, 67, 80, 99–101, 171n21; infrastructure issues, 117; learning curves for new, 87–88; on meeting market demand, 133; Pollan on local, 15; prices for alternative, 21–22; risks for, 87; on social good of their work, 65; sustainability practice of, 56–58; toxicity in corporate, 18–19; zero-waste approach of, 56–57

memoirs. *See* food memoirs

micro farms, 10

micro-sociological traditions, 35

Mikulak, Michael, 8

"Miles to Go before I Eat" (Anderson), 19–20

Minnesota, 46, 139–40

moral batteries, 169n94

moral codes, 26, 33; for chefs and restaurants, 74–84; context and experience role in, 44, 48, 49–50, 53–54, 73, 84; critical environmentalism, 60–61; definition of, 29; emotions and, 40; identity and social action relation to, 48, 156, 157–59; institutional spheres and, 28–29; for legacy and returning farmers, 61–74, 125–26, 157, 170n20; of mushroom hunters, 29; new farmers, 49–61; race and socioeconomics in, 137–39, 157; unique approach to, 39

morality and ethics, 165n6, 166n18; capitalistic markets erosion of, 103; claims compared to reality in local food movement, 25–26, 30; of consumption, 3, 4; context role in social action relation to, 30–34, 48; cultural "tool kit" and social action relation to, 30–31, 168n75; emotions as cues to, 35–36, 40, 69; farmers reliance on, 33–34, 43–44, 47–48, 123–24; fields in explaining social action relation to, 32; food writing on, 14, 16, 17–18, 19; "good farmer," 34, 45–49, 62, 64, 68, 70, 156, 160; habitus in explaining social action relation to, 32, 169n79; interaction ritual chains and, 175n24; local food market sustained by, 2–3, 4–5, 30, 33; local food producers and distributors shared and unique, 10–11,

24–25, 33, 39, 56; Nabhan food memoir use of, 17–18; Pollan on local food movement and, 15; Sayer on social action relation to, 31–32; social action and emotions relation to, 3, 27–32, 35–37, 40, 54, 85, 155–60, 168n75, 169n91, 169n94, 175n24; of social action relation to identity, 31–32, 37, 47; sociology of, 5, 27–28; tales, as type of food writing, 25

moral market, 39; challenges and limits, 172n10, 173n19; characteristics of, 90–91, 102–3, 171n1; consumer participation in, 4, 35, 91, 92, 115; farm size limitations in, 101. *See also* local and alternative food systems

moral order, 60; in capitalistic markets, 29, 171n2; in conventional agriculture, 29–30; defining, 28; ethos and worldview relation to, 28–29; in local and alternative food systems, 3, 4–5, 30, 33, 38, 39; motivations to sustain, 29

Morgan, Caitlin, 160

mushroom producers, 29, 53, 58

Nabhan, Gary, 16–18

narratives. *See* stories and storytelling

Nelson, Paul, 75

networking, 92; challenges and needs, 151–53

new farmers. *See* greenhorn farmers

New York food systems, 1–2, 24, 123, 171n32; dairy farms dominance in, 6; farm-to-table movement and, 77; foodie culture and, 7; local food movement challenges in, 92; market, pre-pandemic, 150–51; market norms for, 102–3; morality and social action at play in, 36–37; motivations for local market in, 27; study demographics and region, 6, 37, 165n11, 169n97; study goals and conclusions, 38; study participants, 37–38; support network for local, 92; young and artisanal producers increase in, 6

niche farms, 10

norms and normativity, 39; capitalistic markets and, 29, 95–96, 103; lay, 27; moral behavior attributed to maintaining, 30; stories role in, 12. *See also* local market creation and norms; moral order

nose-to-tail cooking, 75, 79, 80; educating consumer on, 88, 121–22

The Omnivore's Dilemma (Pollan), 15, 52

organic agriculture and market: certification process and costs, 33, 89, 104; chefs com-

mitment to local over, 80–82; corporate food giants co-opting, 8, 135; pest and weed control in, 55, 105; soil health and, 71–72; store owners and farmer relationships, 134–35; transparency around, 104–5, 115
Otero, Gerardo, 30

packaging, reduction of, 9
pandemic. *See* COVID-19
pastoralism, 14, 26, 168n61
pasture-raised, meaning of, 12
pesticides, 16, 21, 46, 55, 68
pests, 94; organic sprays and methods for, 55, 105
pioneer stories: on cattle ranchers, 21–22; emotional connections to, 23–24; resurrection of protagonist theme in, 23; theme and elements of, 16, 20–21, 23
Pollan, Michael, 14, 15–16, 24, 52
Polletta, Francesca, 13
pollution, 8–9
pork production, 18–19. *See also* meat producers
Press, Melea, 9
prices: alternative meat production and, 21–22; consumer education around, 120–21, 131–32; consumers ability/desire to pay higher, 119–21; profitability and reality of, 1, 137; socioeconomic class and, 97–98, 137–38; supermarkets, competition with, 120, 122–23, 137
profit, 154; chefs' commitment to local farmers over, 82; for conventional compared with small-scale local producers, 6; CSA owners on, 42; farmers attitudinal differences on, 46–47; greenhorn farmers' approach to, 59–60; moral commitment over, 27, 46–47, 84, 105, 156–57; moral market practices and, 91; during pandemic, 142–43; rejection of, as primary goal, 26; working by hand impacts on, 98

quality. *See* taste and quality

race, local food market and, 97–98, 137–39, 157, 169n97
ranchers. *See* meat producers
regenerative agriculture, 101, 172n8
regionalization, 152–53
relationships: chefs cultivation of farmers/suppliers, 9, 75, 76, 77, 81–84, 114–15, 126–27,
157, 171n31; CSAs, with restaurants, 113–15; emotional feedback loop with, 71–72, 159–60; farmers' moral understanding and, 34; foodie culture, 22; in local market creation and norms, 108–15, 172n10; moral code around building and sustaining, 157, 158–59; organic store owners and farmers, 134–35; stories informing our, 12, 13; transparency and trust fostered in, 3, 4, 15, 16, 104–5, 114–15. *See also* consumer relationships; family restaurants, 37; consumer education by, 121–22; cooperative practices and attitudes, 107–8; CSA relationships built with, 113–15; farmer/supplier relationship cultivation for, 126–27; farm-to-table, 9, 74–76, 77, 88, 90, 130, 149; gastropub, 80; legacy/returning farmers selling to, 62; local food adoption pathway for, 76; local food popularity in, 6, 9; local food sourcing dedication of, 22; meat producers price margins and, 117–18; moral codes for, 74–84; nose-to-tail cooking practices of, 75, 79, 80, 88; pandemic and community service of, 147–48; pandemic impacts on, 127, 139, 141, 147–50; taste and quality of local food as drivers for, 74–76; transparency and trust importance for, 83, 114–15. *See also* chefs
returning farmers. *See* legacy and returning farmers
risk, 2, 6, 21, 38, 87, 90

Sage, Colin, 4
Salatin, Joel, 14
Sandstrom, Kent, 31
Sayer, Andrew, 27–28, 31–32, 159
seasonal foods and cuisine, 16, 17; chefs focusing on, 9; consumers understanding of, 130; CSA-restaurant partnership and, 113; in winter, 18–19
self. *See* identity
Silent Spring (Carson), 21, 41
small-scale farming. *See* farm size
Smith, Christian, 27, 28
social action: context impacts on, 30–34; cultural "tool kit" and, 30–31, 168n75; emotions as cues to, 35–36, 40, 69; emotions as "moral batteries" for, 169n94; fields role in morality and, 32–33; health impacts of food producers, 40; identity preservation relation to ethical, 31–32, 37, 47; local food context impact on, 33; moral codes as touchstone for, 48, 156, 157–59;

196 | INDEX

social action (*cont.*)
  morality and emotions relation, 3, 27–32, 35–37, 40, 54, 85, 155–60, 168n75, 169n91, 169n94, 175n24; moral sentiments compared to emotion-based, 36; motivations and shaping forces of, 27; Winchester on embodied action and morality, 159, 170n14
socioeconomics, 169n97; moral codes and, 137–39, 157; prices and, 97–98, 137–38
sociology: economic, 29; morality and, 5, 27–28
soil health/fertility, 95, 159; alternative farmers protection of, 45, 92–93, 172n7; Barber on protecting, 92–93; cattle and, 100–101; challenges, 90, 96–97; crop rotation and cover crops for, 93–94; farm size limits for, 96–97; legacy/returning farmers on, 71–72; local food producers focus on, 93; new farmer focus on, 55–56; pesticides impact on, 46; practices for, 93–94; regenerative agriculture and, 101, 172n8; zone tillage and, 68–69, 171n22
Stets, Jan, 169n91
stewardship: commitment to, 2–3, 45–46, 62–63, 159; contemporary pastoralism and, 168n61; "good farmers" commitment to, 45–46; for legacy/returning farmers, 62–63, 64, 65, 89, 126
Stock, Paul, 34, 47, 60
stores. *See* grocery stores, local focused; supermarkets, conventional
stories and storytelling: emotions and actions triggered with, 13–14, 23–24; morality tales and, 25; moral order of community impacted with, 13; scholars on impacts and significance of, 12, 167n54. *See also* food memoirs; food writing/journalism; pioneer stories
supermarkets, conventional, 15–16, 120, 122–23, 137
sustainability: beliefs about, 2–3, 46; chefs on, 78–79, 80, 121–22; contemporary pastoralism and, 168n61; CSA owner on, 42; defining, 45–46; "good farmers" commitment to, 46; legacy/returning farmers commitment to, 64, 65, 67–68, 69; meat producers' commitment to, 56–57; new farmers' commitment to, 55–56, 58, 59; nose-to-tail cooking practice and, 75, 79; regenerative agriculture role in, 101, 172n8. *See also* soil health/fertility
Swidler, Ann, 30–31, 32, 168n75

Talk of Love (Swidler), 32
taste and quality, 4, 11, 14; chefs' motivation around, 74–76, 77, 80, 82–84; consumer response to, 71–72; farmers' motivation around, 99, 126, 127–28; local food relation to, 9, 10
Tavory, Ivo, 35
Thoits, Peggy, 158
Thompson, Craig, 9, 53
tillage, zone, 68–69, 171n22
transparency. *See* trust and transparency
travelogues, 14, 16
trust and transparency: cheesemakers on, 104–5; farmers' markets norms around, 102, 104, 115; industrial agriculture and food systems lack of, 7–8, 17; local and alternative food systems fostering of, 3, 4, 10, 15, 16, 89, 91, 102–3, 104–5, 114–15, 158; in organic agriculture and market, 104–5, 115; with restaurants and chefs, 83, 114–15
Turner, Jonathan, 169n91

The Unsettling of America (Berry), 21
"The Upstart Cattleman" (Kessler), 21
urban agriculture, 6
USDA: inspections for meat producers, 116; organic certification under, 33, 104; report on local food systems, 5, 6, 123

Vaisey, Stephen, 168m75
Vermont, 18–19, 147

Walmart, 43, 173n22, 174n4
Washington State, food study, 9
Waters, Alice, 9, 14, 75, 78, 171n31
weather, 2, 18–19, 165n1
"weavers" (network builders), 151
Weber, Klaus, 47–48, 67, 171n21
weeds, 55, 94, 105
Weiler, Anelyse, 30
Western Diet, 15
Winchester, Daniel, 159, 170n14
winter, local and seasonal eating in, 18–19
Wittman, Hannah, 30
work load, 26, 96–96, 97, 98
Worster, Donald, 46

zone tillage, 68–69, 171n22

ABOUT THE AUTHOR

STEPHEN ELLINGSON is Professor of Sociology at Hamilton College. He is the author of *To Care for Creation: The Emergence of the Religious Environmental Movement* and *The Megachurch and the Mainline: Remaking Religious Tradition in the Twenty-First Century*. He is a co-author of *The Sexual Organization of the City*.

Printed in the United States
by Baker & Taylor Publisher Services